The Illusion
of Progress
in the Arab World

Galal Amin

The Illusion
of Progress
in the Arab World

A Critique of Western Misconstructions

Translated by David Wilmsen

The American University in Cairo Press
Cairo • New York

Copyright © by Galal Amin
First published in Arabic in 2005 as *Khurafat taqaddum wa ta'akhkhur al-
'arab wa-l-hadara al-'arabiya fi mustahall al-qarn al-wahid wa-l-'ishrin*
Protected under the Berne Convention

Dar el Kutub No. 14060/05
ISBN 977 424 971 2

Designed by Sally Boylan/AUC Press Design Center
Printed in Egypt

Contents

Preface

This book raises many doubts about the belief in 'progress,' i.e., the belief that human history is a history of continuous improvement, with every historical epoch being superior to the one before. It also raises doubts about the belief that some countries or nations are 'advanced' compared with others that are considered to be 'backward,' 'less developed,' or 'lagging behind' and whose primary need is to 'catch up' with the more 'developed' nations. The alleged advance of the West is the main target of discussion in this book in contrast to the alleged lagging behind of the Arabs.

It is not denied that there are important areas of life in which some countries have achieved real progress compared with others. What is denied is that there is such a thing as general or overall progress, or that there are countries that are advanced in a general sense, without specifying the particular areas in which they are ahead of others.

The book begins by arguing that this belief in progress, which is so widespread today, is by no means a very old belief, nor is it self-evident; and some explanations for its emergence and spread are presented (chapter 1). Reasons are given for refusing to measure progress or backwardness by economic indicators alone (chapter 2), as well as to rank some countries ahead of others with regard to what is commonly called human development (chapter 3).

Six other areas are then put forward, in which there is widespread belief that some countries have achieved greater progress than others but where reasons could be given to doubt that such major achievements have indeed been made. These six areas are: freedom, political democracy, economic organization, human rights, the information revolution, and ethics (chapters 4–9).

In chapter 10, the labeling of some countries or nations as more guilty than others of fostering 'terrorism,' is also rejected and the phenomenon of terrorism is analyzed so as to show the true motives behind the international campaign to fight it.

Two well-known books are analyzed in the light of the rejection of the idea of progress, namely Aldous Huxley's *Brave New World* and George Orwell's *1984*, both books being taken as arguing that what is often regarded as progress is really 'progress backward' (chapter 11).

The last chapter admits the existence of a dire need for reform in the Arab world, but distinguishes between the needed 'reform' and the process of 'modernization' that is actually taking place in the name of progress.

1

The Illusion of Progress

Every age has its myths and legends. One of the myths of the modern age is the idea of progress: that human history represents a continuous movement from bad to better, as if climbing the rungs of a ladder, with every rung being not only higher but also better than the one below it. If that were truly the case, then the present must be better than the past, and the future will be better than both.

By belief in the idea of progress, I do not mean simply a belief that with time, humans realize progress in certain things, I mean the belief that humans realize an overall and indiscriminate advance, not in this thing or that, but in their way of life taken as a whole. Nor is it that humans are subject to constant change—for change can involve improvement in some things and disaster in others—but that they are constantly getting better. I maintain that the belief in progress is widespread, almost as if it were part of the air we breathe. It seeps into us through the school curriculum when we are young, we gulp it down in books and in the media, and it is force-fed to us in political speeches and development plans.

We divide history into the early, medieval, and modern periods—the implication being, of course, that the modern is the best of them all—and political systems into traditional,

1

which is to say early, and modern. Moving from the first to the last of these is considered highly desirable. Economic advancement is divided into similar stages. First, there is the traditional stage, followed by a stage of preparation for take-off, by the take-off itself, then by the stage of maturity, and finally the stage of 'mass high consumption,' which is really nothing but the current American lifestyle. Some writers have said lately that with the fall of the Soviet Union and the Socialist bloc, we have reached the end of history. But in his *The End of History and the New Man* Francis Fukuyama[1] does not intend to refute the notion of progress; he just maintains that mankind has finally gained the wisdom necessary to realize that the ideal political and economic regime is that of free markets and liberal democracy of the type currently applied in the United States. He would argue that the future still holds more improvement, albeit not in the arena of ideology or choice of political and economic systems.

Can there be any better description of persons or things than to say that they are 'modern?' By the same token, is there any worse thing to say than that they are reactionary, or behind the times, or swimming against the tide of history, or living in the past? Otherwise, why the huge celebration at the dawn of the twenty-first century and the clamor with which the new century was rung in? Politicians need say little more to inspire reform efforts than to assert the necessity of preparing ourselves for the new century or to say that if we do not do this or that we will slip gradually back into the nineteenth century or even further back into the Middle Ages, while others more diligent will deservedly progress into the twenty-first century.

No doubt, this faith in the idea of progress is strongly related to our intense interest in children. We almost take it for granted that they should be better than we are, and we marvel at them when we see them operating computers with greater skill than we can muster, mastering new types of musical instruments, and recognizing in an instant the different models and makes of automobiles while they treat their elders the way they treat anything out of the past.

Even with art and literature, which are supposed to be less subject to the same measures as objective science and not given such assessments as 'backward' and 'advanced,' it is regarded as high praise of an old painting, an ancient ceramic vase, or a poem composed by a poet of old, to say that it is 'surprisingly modern,' i.e., that it approaches current styles in remarkable ways. Another way of saying this is to indicate that the given piece of art anticipates what follows, or that it is ahead of its time.

We do not usually find this reverence for the future and blind surrender to the concept of progress to any large degree among those with a lower education level and income—indeed, we might not find it there at all. This does not mean that they are simple in judgment or that they are less able to grasp the truth. All it means is that they have not been subjected to the same powerful force-feeding of the doctrine of progress, reverence for the future, and scorn for the past precisely because of their limited education and their restricted access to the mass media and modern culture. This might sound like a praise of illiteracy, but I only wish to call attention to some of the received concepts and articles of faith that comprise contemporary education and with which students are indoctrinated as if they were truths. Among these received concepts is the belief in progress.

So deeply fixed is this notion of progress in our minds that we may be surprised to realize that it is a relatively new concept that we only stumbled upon about five centuries ago, during the European Renaissance. One of the few works that may be said to incorporate the notion of progress prior to the Renaissance was the Arab story of Hayy ibn Yaqzan, told by Ibn Tufayl[2] and written in the twelfth century AD. Even this story however, can be understood to apply the notion of progress to some things and not to others. Nor was the idea of progress inherited from the ancient Greeks, who, for their part, were more inclined to view history as a cycle of improvement and decline, not as a line rising ever upward or a ladder whose rungs lead to higher degrees of refinement.

For its part, Christian thought prevalent in the Middle Ages was closer to regarding human history as a path toward perpetual degradation than as continual betterment. The fourteenth-century Arab writer Ibn Khaldun, often regarded as the father of social science, was close to the ancient Greeks in his view of history as a cycle whose end point was very much the same as its beginning. Both he and the Greek philosophers drew an analogy between human history and the life cycle of an individual human being. A person is born, grows, reaches maturity, and declines into weakness and senility before dying. Then someone new is born and grows to maturity, not necessarily any better than the one before, and that person's fate is also death.

Indeed, the idea of continuous progress is far from being self-evident; on the contrary, simple reflection may bring us to exactly the opposite conclusion. Given what we all observe of the course of individual human life, birth, and growth to maturity followed by decline toward death, we may consider this as the mark of humanity as a whole. There are innumerable examples of human progress, whether in the lives of individuals or in humanity as a whole, in which progress in some areas is realized at the expense of something else. Children may have great powers of imagination, but grown men and women develop their mental reasoning and acquire greater knowledge of facts at the expense of their imaginative capacities. It is well attested that the ability to solve complex mathematical problems does not develop very much beyond the age of twenty, while other mental faculties continue to develop long after. There is also evidence that as children progress through school, they develop some talents at the expense of others. Humans are, after all, limited in their mental as well as physical capacities, and it is hard to imagine that they might develop particular aspects of themselves without incurring costs in other aspects. If that is so for individual humans, why should it not be so for humanity as a whole?

I will here beg the indulgence of the reader to join me in imagining what might pass through the mind of an Arab resident of ninth- or tenth-century Baghdad, when that city was flowering with wealth and culture, were he suddenly transported to our age, took a stroll through the streets of a modern European or American city, and compared the lifestyles of the two periods. I doubt that such a man would pass favorable judgment on everything he saw in a modern city compared to what was familiar in an ancient Arab city.

He would probably approve of the width of the streets and the ease with which they could be navigated, although he might not understand the metal contraptions riding on four rubber tires, or why there is often a single rider behind the wheel when each might hold four or five, and the wide streets are made narrow by ten cars passing abreast. This person from the ninth or tenth century may marvel at the quality of the construction of the neat rows of houses along the streets of a city in Europe or America, although he might find the sameness of their construction boring. So too would he be surprised that no children played in the beautiful gardens surrounding the houses or that days and weeks might pass without his seeing a single person even sitting in those gardens. His surprise would be complete when he was told that the reason for these vacant yards and houses was that people preferred owning more possessions to having more children. He might be startled by the sight of someone running along the streets with quick, measured steps, wearing headphones and listening to music or the news, so keen not to lose time that he could not stop to greet his neighbor if he happened to see him while running.

Our Arab visitor from that ancient age would also find some modern ways of writing letters strange: whoever wants to write a letter can go to a shop specializing in paper products and choose from a variety of cards, a greeting card for a husband 'or wife, son or daughter, grandfather or grandmother, for there is a card for every age and every occasion. All the sender has to do is to choose an appropriate one—the greeting being already printed on the card—and affix a stamp to it.

He might be surprised to see people on Sunday carrying the weekend edition of the newspaper, almost bending under the weight of all the pages of newsprint. He would be told that they were reading the commentary on news of the past week, only to find that most of the pages were full of advertisements for this or that commodity, made more attractive by association with pictures of beautiful women. Even more surprising to him would be to learn that in order to produce all of these newspapers, huge numbers of trees were sacrificed—cut down and converted into paper.

Sport too would seem strange to this visitor from a distant age. If he were invited to a sporting event, like tennis, for example, he would be surprised to find the winners of the event being awarded prizes worth millions of pounds or dollars. The prize money, he would be told, reaches this surprising sum not for any extraordinary effort or singular talent of the competitors but merely because of the size of the television audience for the match. All that is required of the players is to hit a small ball from one square on the ground into another one next to it. If he were then told by way of explanation that a few hours of exercise per day is essential to maintaining good health, but that hardly anyone actually engages in any sort of exercise at all (spending a good part of their time sitting in their automobiles, instead), he might ask himself, why then is all of this money spent to save effort, like that spent on the automobile, for instance, or on a vacuum cleaner instead of a broom, or on a washing machine instead of hand washing?

If he were invited to dinner and saw the knives, forks, and spoons laid out—those implements of refinement and civilization—and asked about their use, he would be told that they keep the hands clean. He might reply that they themselves will become soiled. If he were then told that they could be washed, he might reply that the hands too can be washed before and after eating.

This visiting stranger would certainly see many impressive things. He would observe, for example, the large number of people reading books and magazines while riding public mass transport, from which he would deduce that knowledge of reading, writing, and arithmetic was widespread (although if he were to discover the subjects of many of the books and magazines they were reading he might be a little less impressed). He would undoubtedly be quite impressed to know of the progress achieved in modern society in discovering the causes of diseases and ways of treating them and thus in extending human life, but he would certainly be alarmed to discover the amount of money spent on unnecessary medicines and the number of medicines that are discovered every year to have been doing more harm than good. He may also be bewildered by the workings behind the invention of television, and he might ask what made the widespread use of the device necessary to such an extent.

The visitor would return from his journey with many thoughts in his mind about progress and backwardness, and he would have seen many examples of each. I am not at all sure that he would necessarily reach the conclusion, as we now do, that the country he had visited had a more advanced way of life than his country of more than one thousand years ago.

If that is the case, then how exactly did these ideas of progress and backwardness so indelibly seep into our minds?

The first answer that may come to mind is an old observation of Ibn Khaldun, of the tendency of the conquered to imitate the conqueror. Victory in any field is something to be desired, and this desirability lends to the victor an attractiveness that can render serious flaws invisible. The victors in arms are not necessarily of the best character, the kindest of heart, or the most pleasant to look upon, but the attractiveness they enjoy by means of their power could deceive their beholders into thinking not only that they are the most powerful of people but also the best behaved and most beautiful.

I think this observation by itself is a convincing explanation of the *khawaga*[3] or the foreigner complex (that is, a feeling of inferiority to Europeans or Americans) that many Arabs have, especially when victory is combined with a constant harping by the media commanded by the victors that they possess not only power but all things good. If people are not immediately fooled into thinking that the most powerful is also the best at first sight, then with time and constant trumpeting of this as truth, they likely will be.

If pure unadulterated power were enough to inspire the khawaga complex, then what if power is joined to other desirable advantages, such as material affluence and efficiency? Let us take material affluence first. The same technological advancement with which Europe and then America gained military superiority and then conquered Africa and Asia enabled them also to acquire greater wealth and affluence. This affluence comprises many desirable things: enough food, fine clothing, spacious housing, more leisure, longer vacations—or at least the ability to have more leisure and to take longer vacations. Combine material abundance with military might and the ability to enforce their will over others, and there is nothing easier than gulling people into thinking that all of this must indicate superiority in everything else.

Then add superior efficiency to greater power and wealth. Technological advancement allows more to be done in less time. More goods and services can be produced at lower cost and effort. The free time technological advancement offers also allows for greater scientific advancement and greater skill in the production of art, literature, and philosophy. Again, there is nothing easier than to dupe people into thinking that the increased efficiency of production must also mean an advanced social order, greater freedom, and a higher level of humanity in general, not just in material ways.

Thus the belief has spread and persisted, as if it has seeped into our pores, that enhanced power, material affluence, and efficiency must mean advancement in all aspects of life: social cohesion and political organization, morality and beauty, and human welfare in all of its elements, be they material or otherwise. So when the person who possesses the power, material abundance, and efficiency is a foreigner, a *khawaga*, we are struck with the khawaga complex.

That goes a long way toward explaining why the educated, in general, are more afflicted with the khawaga complex than others. Even though the entire nation shares in the costs of colonialism and foreign exploitation of its resources, the educated in any nation are usually those who undertake direct dealings with foreigners, taking orders from them or complying with their requests, acting as intermediaries between them and their countrymen, and mixing with them in leisure-time entertainment at parties and clubs. The educated, more than others, are exposed to the foreigners' power and authority and know the extent of their wealth and opulence, while the simpler and poorer folk of the nation know of this only by hearsay.

By mixing with foreigners, through exposure in the schools and universities, and indeed through direct experience if they get a chance to go abroad for study, work, or pleasure, the educated see with their own eyes what foreigners have achieved by way of knowledge, technological advance, and efficiency, while their countrymen hear of it only in stories that are quickly forgotten. Nevertheless, the matter is not limited simply to witnessing, but extends to something more important and altogether graver: remuneration. The educated members of the population of a foreign-occupied country do not just take the orders from foreigners and convey them to others, they are also the ones who get the rewards and the kickbacks. In order to guarantee their loyalty, the foreign powers have to furnish them with some of the same comforts that they themselves enjoy. The educated elites are thus allowed to taste exactly what advanced technology can bring by way of a comfortable life, to be introduced to a great variety of goods of which the rest of the population has not even dreamed. How can the will of the educated fail to weaken in the face of such power on the one hand and such rewards on the other? Their will does weaken, their morals relax. Little by little, they backslide in their dedication to tradition, and they begin to allow themselves to engage in behavior that would otherwise be thought reprehensible. As much as they are able to, they ape the foreigners, and they are often ready to follow them in ridiculing the customs of their countrymen.

———

In the rush of this miserable process of psychological transformation, many valuable things are lost which have no obvious connection with either greater strength and military might or with scientific and technological progress. Where is the connection between building military power or scientific advancement and whether your religion is closer to the truth than mine, whether your language is more refined than mine, your golden-age literature more beautiful or your music more capable of arousing feelings, your people better humored or faster at improvising or more eloquent, your relations with women more humane or your love of children greater than mine? What is the relationship between military might, material well-being, or technological advancement and whether you are quicker to forgive than I, more or less able to control your emotion when angry . . . and so on?

Yes, there is a connection, but it is much more complex than we might imagine. Material well-being can indeed permit you to be less fanatical in your attitude to religion and more tolerant of other religions. This, however, is only one factor limiting the degree of fanaticism or tolerance. More important perhaps than greater material well-being in delimiting these are other considerations such as the spread of consumer-culture values, sharper competitiveness, and the degree of contentment with what has been achieved of that material well-being.

True, a rise in the level of well-being permits more leisure time, which might lead to greater skill in literary and artistic production, but this will not necessarily happen. Greater material wealth makes more leisure time possible but not inevitable. Indeed, we see many wealthy countries where the people prefer more goods to more free time, and we often see people in much poorer countries enjoying more leisure time. In any case, why should greater productivity and excellence in literature and art not hinge upon other factors that might be more important than longer leisure time? And could it not be that greater leisure allowed to the elite is more conducive to a higher level of art than greater leisure to the masses? Consider, for example, what happened to Russian literature from the mid-nineteenth century to the mid-twentieth century, despite the increase in well-being in the society as a whole. Rapid economic and technological developments achieved by Soviet Russia have certainly not produced finer literature than was produced under the tsars. Again, consider the effect of a spreading consumer culture in the West on the quality of literature and art–there are many who would claim that literature and art indeed have declined in quality as a direct result of the spread of consumerism among the teeming masses. What we have gained in quantity, we may have lost in quality. Bad art and literature, like bad money, could easily drive out the good.

Are we really capable of delineating clearly and determining the effect of technological advancement on aspects of life like art and literature, language and eloquence, the degree of freedom and democracy, the potential for war or peace, social cohesion, morality, religious faith, the ability to communicate intimately and naturally, and so on? It was long thought, and the effect of that belief is still with us, that raising the level of education among all classes must result in a higher level of morality. This was the view of the Enlightenment thinkers in the eighteenth century and the socialists of the succeeding centuries. Now we find to our surprise that morality levels follow rules of their own only loosely tied to the advancement of knowledge or the spread of education. As for the influence of technological progress, who can say with certainty whether the social effects of the automobile, the television, the cinema, the mobile telephone, or the Internet have been desirable or not?

It must then be admitted that the link between greater power, material wealth, scientific or technological advance, and progress and backwardness in other aspects of life is far from being obvious. Nevertheless, there is nothing easier than to fall into the trap of imagining that there is such a necessary link. The trick is not very different from the trick played by the seller who lures you into buying some trivial thing that you have no need for by displaying it in an attractive box, or by using a pretty face to sell it to you. You then irrationally associate the beauty of the seller or the color of the box with the quality of what is inside.

It is worth noting that for the Egyptians, the khawaga complex is not something of long vintage. Rather, the phenomenon hardly goes farther back than a hundred years. I have no doubt that my grandfather did not suffer from such a complex in the slightest, nor indeed did my mother. My father, however, would have been afflicted by the disease to some degree. He then passed it on to me and to my siblings, and I probably passed it on to my children. But this story needs some fleshing out.

My grandfather was born in the middle of the nineteenth century, that is, about a third of a century before the British occupation of Egypt. The occupation came as a shock to him and to his generation. They could not believe that infidels could with such ease plant their feet on Muslim soil and impose their will over a people who believed in Allah and his Messenger, and who owed allegiance to the Muslim sultan in Istanbul. My grandfather could find no explanation for this state of affairs except that Egyptians must have departed from the true faith and denied the obligations that Allah had placed upon them. Thus came the punishment of Allah in the form of British power over them. This was the clear and simple view of my grandfather, and it invited no discussion. When my father once asked him whether the English believed in Allah too and whether that was why they gained victory over us, my grandfather rebuked him and refused to answer.

What is sure is that my grandfather never for a single instant lost confidence that he and his nation were superior to those foreigners who, but for their rifles and cannons, were no better than we were in any way. Indeed, he considered himself and his nation more fortunate for having been born Muslims, while the English had not.

My grandfather's complete self-confidence is not hard to explain. Yes, the English possessed greater military might and there was no doubt that the European standard of living was higher than that of the Egyptians, even in my grandfather's day. But what did my grandfather see as demonstrations of this power throughout his life? How many of the trappings of comfort and the life of ease that foreigners enjoyed did he witness? What did he experience of the effects of advanced science and technology? The answer is very little indeed.

The percentage of Egyptians who had direct contact with foreigners throughout most of my grandfather's life, that is, from the middle of the nineteenth century until the start of the First World War, remained extremely small. It cannot have been more than two or three percent of the entire population, considering the small number of foreigners coming to Egypt at the time and their concentration in the larger cities. To be sure, the economic policy imposed on Egypt by the occupation had an important effect on the lives of all Egyptians, but that is one thing and direct observation and personal contact is quite another. True, my grandfather was an educated man, but his education, like that of the great majority of educated Egyptians in those days, was a religious education gained at al-Azhar University,[4] which prevented my grandfather, as it prevented most Egyptians, from entertaining any doubt about his faith or way of life.

As for technology, what could my grandfather have known or heard of its advance? He did not listen to the radio except occasionally toward the end of his life. He did not know about the telephone. And he never saw a film in his life. He did not read the newspaper daily, as had become common practice, and he lived most of his life without electric lights. If he rode the tramway, it was for most of his life a horse-drawn tram, and riding one was itself considered a big event. It scarcely needs mentioning that my grandfather never left Egypt, so he never observed how foreigners lived in their own lands and he probably never met anyone who might have described their lifestyle to him. Indeed, what would the Europeans themselves have known of any of this before the beginning of the 1930s, when my grandfather died? Many of the common comforts and conveniences of today were unknown to anyone in those days, and most of what was available was restricted to a very small percentage of non-Egyptians, even in their own countries. So where could the khawaga complex have possibly come from?

Where this khawaga complex is concerned, my mother's situation was very close to that of my grandfather. She was a traditional woman in every sense of the word. She knew very little of the West, and she enjoyed fewer of the modern conveniences and means of entertainment than even my grandfather did. She never traveled further westward or northward than Alexandria. She knew no more than six or seven words of a foreign language, all of them rhyming (cat, rat, sat, fat), which she never spoke except in jest. She never felt she was missing anything.

I am certain that she, like my grandfather, felt in no way lesser than the English, nor did she feel that she was better than them. When one of my elder brothers married an Austrian girl and came home with her to Egypt, I never noticed in my mother anything that indicated that she felt that the European woman was any better than she. All she ever did was to express her commiseration with the young woman who came to live in Egypt so far away from her mother in Austria and with the mother whose daughter had traveled so far from her.

There were perhaps only two things wrong with Europe as far as my mother could see: the first was the extreme cold that she heard about from my brother, who had gone to study there, and the second was that the few Europeans she came across in Egypt cooked without *samna balady*,[5] which in her view noticeably ruined the taste of the food that Europeans ate and very much reduced its nutritional value. Aside from these two things, I think my mother's feelings toward Europeans or foreigners in general were no different from those expressed by the narrator in the famous novel by Tayeb Salih, *Season of Migration to the North*. When the narrator returned to his village in the Sudan and the villagers would ask him whether the Europeans were any better than they, he would answer, "They are just like us, they are born and die, and in the journey from the cradle to the grave they dream dreams, some come true and some are frustrated."[6]

My father, who lived until the mid-twentieth century, experienced much greater self-doubt than did my grandfather. For one thing, he had much closer contact with the fruits of modern technology. He had a radio in his house and a refrigerator (even though the latter did not arrive until after he turned sixty). He knew what it was to fly in an airplane (even though he did it no more than twice and only toward the end of his life). He observed the French, English, Swiss, and Dutch in their own countries and saw what it meant to live in an industrialized country, even though he was seeing these things just after the end of the Second World War, when those countries were still paying the price of war, rebuilding what had been destroyed, and the people could obtain many goods only with ration cards. More important, the number of Egyptians who had direct contact with foreigners in Egypt, or at least with a foreign lifestyle, increased several times over between the beginning and the middle of the twentieth century. This was not only because of the increase in the number of foreigners living and working in Egypt, but also because of the growth of the middle class, which had many reasons to remain in contact with foreigners in buying and selling merchandise, in banks and firms, at schools and universities, at sporting clubs and other places of recreation. In all of these meeting places, Egyptians would see things to dazzle the eye and enchant the heart. They would see the European way of concluding deals and the way Europeans conducted themselves in earnest and at play. When they connected all of that to the foreigners' higher standard of living and their capability in enforcing their will over the Egyptians, their admiration and respect increased, even if they made the connection grudgingly. Indeed, my father gave voice to this feeling in his autobiography, when he described an Arabic teacher whom he admired greatly at the age of eighteen. After heaping praise upon the teacher, my father wrote, "The students called him the 'English Sheikh' because of his haughty and free manner as well as his candor in speaking and his breadth of thought."[7]

The type of education my father received, compared to that of my grandfather, must have had an influence on his view of foreigners, which no doubt reinforced the khawaga complex in him. Nor can my grandfather be considered completely blameless in that. True, he himself was largely immune to this complex, but it seems that some doubt began to grip him when he considered whether the education he had received was also the best for his son. He must have been hearing about the opening of schools that applied modern methods of education. Aside from the sources of Islamic law, Arabic grammar, and some mathematics, the new schools taught modern sciences which he thought might have some benefit, even if only in the service of religion. He began asking people whom he regarded as having good judgment and sound views whether it might not be better to send his son to one of these modern schools than to send him to the same sort of institution where he himself had been educated. After he had heard every manner of opinion, he started taking my father out of one type of school, enrolling him in the other, and then returning him to the first type. This meant that my father was struck with severe confusion in his early years of schooling, when he was obliged to change his school clothes time after time from the Azhari headdress and caftan to the civilian shirt and trousers and back again, suffering the scorn of some of his classmates—especially those who studied at the modern schools—if they happened to see him, still a small boy, wearing the headdress and caftan of a sheikh. This scorn must have left its mark on him, and perhaps that was the very origin of the khawaga complex in him.

If this first shock was associated with something solely material—clothing—more important perhaps were the purely intellectual shocks to which my father was later exposed. The greatest of these was his realization that the writings of some Orientalists on the history of Islam may be better than those of many Muslim historians. To quote again from his autobiography:

One day I met a friend and we went to a coffee shop. The talk strayed from the arts to a book in English, *Theology of Islam*, by an American Orientalist named McDonald. The author had divided his book into three sections, one addressing governance in Islam, one on Islamic jurisprudence, and one on the various creeds and schools of thought in Islam. He spoke so highly of the book that I found myself suddenly asking him: "Can you come with me right now to the Berlitz School so I can enroll in an English class?" He agreed, and I swore I would learn English so that I could read that book.[8]

Many similar shocks must have followed and my father no doubt tried as best he could to reconcile himself to them. While he was learning English, however, he maintained his sense of loyalty to and respect for the Arabic language. He employed the scientific method in his study of Islam while maintaining his faith and his devotion to his religion. He went on to teach Arabic literature in the Faculty of Literature at the Egyptian university, but he gave up the Azhari dress in accordance with the climate of the new university, which took European universities as its model.

Nevertheless, and despite all his tireless efforts to combine his adoption of some western ways with loyalty to tradition, I think my father was unable to free himself entirely from the khawaga complex. He was never able to deliver himself from it the way my grandfather and my mother were, or rather he was exposed to a danger that they were really never exposed to. The contagion was inevitably passed on to me and my siblings, and had become much more severe when it was transferred from us to the next generation.

2

Economic Development

Before 1950, the term 'economic development' was hardly ever used to describe the goal of the poorer countries of the world, and literature on the subject under any rubric was rare. This was the period of classic imperialism, characterized by the usurping of raw materials produced by the colonized countries, the exploitation of their cheap labor, and the marketing of finished products produced by the colonial countries. The goals of this kind of colonialism hardly needed any economic development in the colonized countries in the way we now understand the term (higher income, greater industrialization, higher labor productivity, etc.). In fact, the goals of colonialism were mostly in direct conflict with economic development in these countries, since development implied increased wages (something that the colonial powers did not want), increased manufacturing using local raw materials (also undesirable), and the production of goods for import substitution (which would slam the door in the face of the exports of colonial countries).

In this situation, it was quite convenient to circulate the notion among the population of the colonized countries that their economic development was a nearly impossible task. A number of reasons were given for this, the most important of which was the contention that their culture prevented them from achieving such a lofty goal. Their national culture was said to inculcate a fatalistic attitude to life, excessive respect for the past, resistance to change, imposing a spiritual dimension on things purely economic, fostering the extended family at the expense of the spirit of individualism, and maybe hostility to, or even a prohibition of, charging interest on loans. All of these things would hinder economic development; indeed, they would positively prevent it. So it was better for the 'backward countries,' as they were often called at the beginning of the twentieth century, to forget industrialization and be content with what they had.

By the middle of the twentieth century, the world had changed greatly from what it had been a century, or even a half-century earlier. In the poor countries, various forms of economic progress came to be welcomed by the developed countries. New types of goods—from automobiles and Coca-Cola to armaments—were now searching for new markets, including the markets of much poorer countries. The marketing of such goods in poor countries required a certain amount of development, leading to an increase in average incomes, on condition that such an increase did not bring about in the poor countries the ability to produce such goods themselves, thus reducing the need to import them. Rather than continuing to allege that economic development in these countries was impossible, the slogans of development started spreading like wildfire after the end of the Second World War. But since some kind of development was now desirable, it seemed more appropriate to cease calling these countries backward and to use the more optimistic term 'underdeveloped' or, even better, 'developing.' National cultures were no longer regarded as prohibiting economic development, but still they were considered an obstruction slowing down the process. The hope for economic change was supported and encouraged, but national cultures had to be adapted appropriately.

Authors who addressed the subject of economic development during the 1950s and 1960s found it easy to talk about what was then called the 'common characteristics of underdeveloped countries.' These were not limited to economic characteristics such as low per capita income, low productivity, or the dominance of agriculture, but included several cultural characteristics as well. Not one good word was said about these cultural characteristics, and the possibility that they may enhance human welfare and may even, under certain circumstances, be favorable to economic development was hardly ever considered. Strong family ties, for instance, or loyalty to tradition may produce positive results, not only in bringing about greater equity but also in discouraging wasteful consumption and boosting saving and investment.

Throughout the 1950s and 1960s, another insult was addressed to the national cultures of poor countries, which was to lump them all together in one group without caring much about bringing out the important differences between one culture and another as long as they all shared in those undesirable qualities that had been called the 'characteristics of underdeveloped countries. Where those characteristics are concerned, India was like China, the Arabs were like the Africans and Latin Americans, and Muslims were not different from pagans. After all, do they not all have low per capita income when compared to the United States?

At that time, one of the most popular theories about economic development was Walt Rostow's theory of the stages of economic development, which placed any country on a scale of five levels.[9] The goal, of course, was to reach the level already reached by the United States, that of high mass consumption, of which the most important feature is widespread consumption of durable goods like automobiles, refrigerators, and vacuum cleaners. We students of development were too preoccupied at the time in trying to determine at which stage Rostow would place a particular country, or whether the investment rate he required to move a country from one stage to another was net or gross, to notice that the entire book hardly contained a word about the cultural characteristics of a nation or about what might happen to a culture as the country moved from one of the five stages to another. Perhaps Rostow took it as a presupposition not needing discussion, as Marx had before him, that moving from a backward economic stage to an advanced one must also mean moving from an inferior culture to a superior one.

From the end of the 1960s through the 1970s, a new concept spread in the development literature, propagated by what was known as the 'dependency school,' which called for underdeveloped countries to 'de-link' from the developed countries and to pursue 'self-reliant' development. It is noteworthy that the great majority of writers in this school built their denouncements of dependency on an economic foundation while cultural dependency was usually ignored. Perhaps the explanation for this is that most of the leaders of the dependency school were from Latin America and so came largely from the same Western cultural milieu, sharing a Western language and religion and very similar values and patterns of behavior.

In the 1970s, some writers and international organizations raised the banner of the satisfaction of 'basic needs' as an alternative to increasing per capita income, and started calling attention to the fact that average income may rise while some of the most urgent needs continue to be unsatisfied. Nevertheless, those basic needs whose fulfillment was now advocated were usually limited to material needs like food, clothing, and shelter. It was very rare to find any indication that human beings have cultural needs alongside material needs and that the national culture needs protection just as surely as humans need adequate food, clothing, and shelter. In the 1970s, some also expressed alarm at the deterioration of the environment, warning that rapid economic development threatened the natural environment with pollution and some plant and animal species with extinction. But it was rare to find someone expressing alarm over the fact that the cultures of some poor countries were also facing the danger of extinction.

Then two new catchphrases, 'structural adjustment' and 'globalization,' were added to development vocabulary. They were both used as part of the efforts urging poorer countries to open their doors wide to international trade and foreign investment and of shrinking the role of the state in protecting domestic production and those among its citizens with particularly low incomes. We also began to hear about the need for strengthening civil society and for showing greater respect for human rights, both couched in terms of confronting the power of the state. Civil society was to be strengthened at the expense of state power, and human rights were to be defended against the excesses of the state. The fact is, however, that while the state might indeed commit excesses against individual rights, its input may also be necessary for the protection of some other rights, as when the state guarantees the right to employment to the otherwise unemployable.What is more, state power may be used not merely to protect the economy from competing foreign imports and capital, it may also be necessary for the protection of national culture. The weakening of the role of the state brought about by the sweeping and comprehensive changes called for by these new slogans meant leaving the national culture defenseless against a torrential flood of foreign goods and services, companies, and satellite television channels, adding a new insult to the injury inflicted upon national culture by the development of the 1950s and 1960s.

———

In the 1990s, yet another slogan was raised to suit the new international situation after the fall of the Soviet Union and the beginning of what looked like the United States' exclusive control of the affairs of the world. Opinion makers in the United States hatched the phrase 'clash of civilizations' to take the place of 'combating the danger of communism.' We suddenly found our culture, whether defined as Muslim, Arab, or Egyptian, being described as being in a 'clash' with that of the West, which was of course assumed to be more worthy of survival. The strange thing is that we fell into the trap yet again, failing to note that the condition of the world may not be so much that of a clash of civilizations as an attack by one culture upon another. To characterize the situation as a clash was to imply that there was a genuine struggle between two cultures, that parity in strength existed between the two, with each possessing similar weaponry, and that as a result, either one had an equal possibility of defeating the other, which is of course a gross misrepresentation of the facts.

As if all this were not enough, our national culture is now being described not just as backward or underdeveloped but as breeding terrorists. What is now called for is not merely to elevate the culture by adapting it to the demands of economic development, but to rip it out by the roots. The great outcome, then, of this journey of fifty years since we assumed the good will of the sloganeers of economic development, never objecting when they treated our culture as an obstacle to development, is to reach a point where our culture is considered not merely a fertile breeding ground for terrorism, but almost synonymous with it.

3

Human Development

In 1990, a U.N. agency, known as the United Nations Development Programme (UNDP), announced its adoption of a new system of ranking the countries of the world, according to which progress or backwardness would be measured by a combination of three indicators, namely 1) per capita income, 2) life expectation at birth, and 3) the level of education.

The first was borrowed from the old widely used indicator of economic development; the second was chosen as an indicator of nutritional status and the state of health; and the third was included on the assumption that it measures important aspects of human welfare and intellectual development.

It is easy to criticize this new measure by observing that it continues to ignore other important factors in human welfare such as the rate of unemployment or the degree of equality in income distribution. It also ignored anything that has to do with culture. For that reason, it may not be regarded as such a great improvement on the previous one, which measured progress and backwardness in terms of per capita income alone. One may also note the harm involved in giving this measure the grand name of 'human development.' As much as we may object to taking per capita income alone as a measure of all progress, at least its proponents were modest enough to admit that it did not encompass all aspects of economic, let alone human progress. On the other hand, to name this new measure human development lends it weight, in that it now speaks to various aspects of human well-being, which is untrue.

Twelve more years passed and suddenly in 2002, there appeared a strange report from the same U.N. agency, the UNDP, but with its focus on the Arab world alone, and bearing the imposing title of *Arab Human Development Report*. This report boldly claimed to present an even more accurate measure of human progress and backwardness. It proposed to do away completely with per capita income and to rely upon three other indicators, those being freedom or democracy, the state of knowledge, and what it called 'the empowerment of women.' Then it set about comparing the Arab states to each other and with other countries, using these three measures.

It looks therefore as if, in the space of fifty or sixty years, we have moved from economic development to human development, and with each step the term development seems to have become more and more odious, and harder to swallow. The source of the trouble may be the fact that the term development evokes in the mind the idea of an increase in numbers, in size, or in other material attributes that are easy to measure. Wealth can be 'developed' by putting aside penny upon penny or adding acre upon acre of land. Animal wealth can be 'developed' by an increase in livestock. But to talk about 'human development' can only lead to confusion and might be used deliberately to mislead. It reduces enormously complex and multifaceted issues to exceedingly simple, and superficial variables with the sole merit of being easier to measure.

Take freedom as an example. Freedom can be restricted by the state, religious institutions, common custom, the head of the household, the clan leader, the party, or the censor, as well as by poverty, disease, disability, old age and so on. If that is the case, how is it possible that one can claim that freedom may be measured by say, the number of times voters go to the ballot box, without even considering whether the parties have distinguishable platforms, or by the number of political prisoners?

A similar thing may be said about the state of knowledge. The goal of increasing knowledge, to the extent that it is a worthwhile goal, is also complex and multifaceted, and to be more knowledgeable is an attribute that is not easily measured. Knowledge is not simply the sum of all pieces of information—otherwise the computer would be the most knowledgeable of all creatures and an encyclopedia would be more knowledgeable than its owner. Increasing knowledge may also be of little use if it reduces the ability to distinguish between that which is of importance and that which is not. It is, therefore, not enough to content ourselves with the sheer increase of knowledge, let alone of information; we must also consider what type of knowledge is involved.

The situation is no less clear in the arena of enhancing the status of women, or to use the term employed by the UNDP report, of greater 'empowerment of women.' It seems to me absurd to take for granted that women in a technologically or economically advanced society necessarily enjoy greater freedom than they enjoy in less technologically advanced societies. Greater empowerment of women in one area may easily reduce their power in other areas of life. Thus, empowering women with money may lead to their loss of independence vis-à-vis the companies from which they earn their money, and empowering women vis-à-vis their husbands could lead to their losing the ability to enjoy motherhood, and so on. In any case, it seems much wiser to avoid the use of the term human development as an indicator of only one or a few improvements that might be associated with several losses in other aspects of human welfare.

There are many aspects of freedom just as there are many types of oppression, and history is full of examples where people have rid themselves of one type of oppression only to replace it with another. We should not let a country's success in economic and technological advancement blind us to its failure to achieve advancement in other aspects of human life. Yet we unfortunately seem to be prone to that error. Our error here is not unlike that of members of a tribe who have been defeated and utterly crushed by another, but notice that the members of the victorious tribe have much larger noses than theirs. They mistakenly come to think that there is a strong connection between their defeat and the size of the nose and hence try to do all they can to enlarge their noses, to the extent of even fixing artificial noses to their faces, with the hope that this may grant them greater strength!

–2–

The second *Arab Human Development Report*, which appeared in August 2003, with the subtitle "Building a

34

Knowledge Society," was released in two versions, in English and in Arabic. I read the Arabic version, but I found the aroma of translation wafting from sentence to sentence. It seemed to me almost certain that although the writers of the report were Arab, they wrote it, or at least a good part of it, first in English and then gave it to someone to translate it into Arabic. The translation may be precise but even so, I think that Arab readers would not be able to understand many parts of it unless they first have access to the English original. Also lamentable is the fact that Arab writers whose goal is to promote knowledge in the Arab world found it necessary or easier to write their report first in English. Perhaps the reason is that they often think in English or, perhaps that they thought it necessary, if they were to communicate with some of their Arab colleagues, to write in English. Or maybe they were mainly addressing the foreign institutions that financed the report, or had lost confidence in the ability of the Arabic language to express their ideas, and so they sought some other language. Whatever the reason, it is certainly a sad situation which must make one feel nostalgic for the days when the writings on Arab reform, whether the discussion was about the state of knowledge or any other subject, were done by such men as Muhammad Abduh or Taha Husayn who thought only in Arabic, discussed things with their colleagues in Arabic, were full of confidence in the ability of the Arabic language to express whatever they wanted to say, and could write and publish what they wrote without the financial support of a U.N. agency. But more important than the language used is the adoption of foreign biases as if they were our own and the defense of foreign interests as if they were our own interests.

35

Take, for example, the subject of freedom and democracy, which is the most oft-repeated theme of this report whether in giving a diagnosis of a problem, in explaining it, or in making recommendations to solve it. In terms of diagnosis, the first problem with the state of knowledge in the Arab world mentioned by the report is the prevalence of "authoritarianism" and "overprotectiveness" in child-raising practices.[10] In discussing the mass media, the first thing the report mentions, after complaining of the low level of circulation of newspapers in the Arab world, is that "most Arab countries live in an environment of severe restrictions on press freedom and freedom of expression . . . and the dominance of the official press presenting a single point of view." When speaking of the production of knowledge in the humanities and the social sciences, the first thing the report complains of is "political and legal interference . . . by drawing red lines around research in these areas." When it comes to literary production, the report complains that "the message of creative artists reaching people through books and the mass media is obstructed by the lack of freedom." The report also adds that, in the view of faculty members of the universities, the radio and television "do not enjoy sufficient freedom."

So much for the diagnosis. Where explanation is concerned, the report emphasizes that the value system in the Arab world does not encourage the spread of knowledge, but it does not fail to mention that the political, social, and economic conditions play an important role in the formation of this value system, "so, the boundaries of freedom remain limited . . . and oppression and marginalization combine to kill the desire for accomplishment, happiness, and participation, leading to apathy and political despair, thus the distancing of citizens from participation in effecting the desired changes."[11]

When it comes to making recommendations, the report has little to say other than to call, again, for "freedom of opinion and expression guaranteed by proper governance."

What can one say to all this? Would anyone deny the importance and benefits of freedom in all spheres of life, including the sphere of knowledge? Certainly not, and one may even ask whether such an important but obvious fact still needs to be rediscovered and emphasized. The question is not whether freedom is important or needed, it is rather whether the lack of freedom is really the most important cause of the low state of knowledge in the Arab world. Freedom is undoubtedly a great thing, and so is better and greater knowledge, but unfortunately these two marvelous things do not always march hand in hand. Greater freedom may be acquired while the state of knowledge is deteriorating if it happens that it is the masses that dictate the state of knowledge, take over the mass media, demand that the educational system cater to their taste, and that they enjoy complete freedom in what they can watch on television or the cinema. In contrast, under an authoritarian ruler who is also enlightened, the state of knowledge may very well advance greatly. This has happened in some periods of Arab history, as well as in some western countries. The famous universities of Europe, such as Oxford or Cambridge, were not established under a flourishing democracy but under the rule of an absolute monarch. The founder of modern Egypt, Muhammad 'Ali, began the system of sending scholars to Europe, and this practice was continued by Gamal 'Abd al-Nasser, but neither of them was a democratic ruler. The state of knowledge deteriorated under their successors, who were more democratic. The age of the flowering of Arab and Islamic thought that the report points to was not an age characterized by democratic rule but by autocracy.

The authors of the report might have benefited by a comparison of the state of knowledge in India and China in the last fifty years, in which India enjoyed a system that is much more democratic than that of China but did not show any noticeable superiority over China in the progress of 'knowledge.' Or it might have been useful if the authors of the report had distinguished between various types of knowledge—scientific, literary, and artistic—or between scientific research and the mere collecting of facts, or between the spread of knowledge through school textbooks and its spread through television, as well as if they had discussed the possible relationship between the growth of each of these types of knowledge and the degree of democratization or the various types of democracy. It looks as if the writers' enthusiasm for democracy of any type, and their great hurry to publish their report in the political climate of the world prevailing today, unfortunately prevented them from drawing such important distinctions and from making such useful comparisons.

Their unjustifiable hurry to cheer for democracy and freedom led the authors of the UNDP report to commit the grave error of ignoring many other impediments to freedom. Readers of the report cannot help but come away with the impression that freedom has only two enemies: authoritarian rule and religious extremism. The first closes mouths and imposes a single opinion on everyone, restricts discussion and dialogue, and suppresses creativity. The second forbids individual attempts at a free interpretation of religion and prohibits what religion does not, such as certain types of scientific inquiry and literary and artistic production, under the pretext that they conflict with the precepts of religion. It also restricts contact with outsiders on the pretext that they are infidels. Such restrictions of the interplay of ideas and the exchange of knowledge and experience must certainly hamper scientific progress and artistic expression.

All of this may be true, but it is missing something important. Readers of this report on the ill effects of authoritarianism and its restrictions on freedom will get the impression that the authoritarian ruler must come from inside the region. If the region is Arab, then the authoritarian ruler must also be Arab. The report ignores how foreign rule may also constitute a threat to various forms of freedom and hence also to the advance of knowledge. For example, in chapter 8 of the report, entitled "The Political Context," in which readers might expect to find a discussion of the various political impediments to freedom and the advancement of knowledge, the report does not include a single sentence on the authoritarian rule created by foreign occupation of Arab lands. This glaring omission happens to be especially surprising at this particular time. Arabs are living through a critical period, characterized by the presence of foreign troops and the occupation of Iraq (to say nothing of the long Israeli maltreatment of the

Palestinians and the recent intensification of that mistreatment). Why are these not mentioned as one of the impediments both to freedom and to the advancement of knowledge in Arab countries? Must the ill effects on the state of knowledge in Iraq necessarily be of Iraqi doing and not of American or British origin?

Extremism is undoubtedly another impediment to the advance of knowledge and creativity, especially when it goes beyond a certain limit, but one must also admit that there are some kinds of extremism which can be beneficial to creativity and knowledge as long as they do not cross certain boundaries. Artists are closer to being extremist in one sense of the word than are people of few talents, and brilliant scientists may owe their brilliance to some kind of extremism in their scientific pursuits. They may even have the appearance of religious fervor about them. Of course, this is not what the writers of the report mean by extremism; what they have in mind is only religious extremism, obviously because of its relationship to what is called terrorism, which happens to be the favorite subject in the mass media nowadays.

But some may like to attract attention to something very much like religious fervor or extremism growing in America after September 11, 2001, which has also had some disastrous effects on the state of knowledge in America and in the outside world. We cannot expect, nor do we wish to see, the writers of the *Arab Human Development Report* delve into American extremism and its effect on knowledge when they are mainly concerned with Arab extremism and its effects on knowledge in the Arab countries. Nevertheless, does that other form of

40

extremism not deserve at least a sentence from them, especially as it does affect the state of knowledge in the Arab world as well? The writers of the report did not neglect to refer to the loss to the Arab world following the events of September 11 as a result of the restrictions placed on Arabs entering the United States, which has led, according to the report, to the loss of access to American knowledge. They might have written at least a small paragraph about how Arabs have been restricted from gaining access to other kinds of knowledge as a result of the American and British occupation of Iraq, and how this new American extremism has led to the silencing of many voices in the Arab countries which may have been beneficial to hear. This has had a stifling effect on independent thought in the same way that religious extremism does. Just as religious extremists decry any *igtihad* (which could be defined as 'the exerting of one's self to the utmost to form an opinion')[12] in the interpretation of religious texts and call for it to be banned, so do American extremists view any *igtihad* at individual interpretation of the events of September 11 as conspiracy theory and call for it also to be banned.

All this, however, does not exhaust the impediments to freedom. Neither authoritarianism, whether internal or imposed from abroad, nor religious or political extremism constitute all the possible impediments to freedom and all possible obstacles to the advance of knowledge. Business interests may also have an adverse effect on the state of knowledge, about which the report is completely silent.

Motivated by the desire to maximize profits, erroneous information is often published by big corporations, not just concerning the goods and services they produce but also concerning the policies they endorse or hold in disfavor, or regarding heads of countries standing in the way of their interests and whose reputations they would like to sully or whom they would like to overthrow. If such interests have anything to do with the sale of arms, there is no end to the brainwashing to which they might resort in order to provoke the outbreak of war or to aggravate the conditions of war if they already exist. In the current era, the monopoly of business interests is growing to the extent that they not only exercise control over the traditional mass media but also extend their influence into the educational system. Little by little, the state is losing ground before the juggernaut of these monopolies.

One would have thought that the UNDP report being discussed should have been more interested in the future than in the past; indeed, the subtitle "Building a Knowledge Society" seems to look toward the future. One would have expected, then, that it would talk about current and future challenges, the most important of which may be the threat posed by such commercial interests. The report should therefore have been much more concerned about such threats to knowledge than about the dangers of authoritarian governments, which may have once posed the main threat to various kinds of knowledge (such as those of the Stalinists or the Nazis) or about the danger of religious extremism, which constituted the main threat to various types of knowledge in medieval Europe. The Arab countries are indeed increasingly subjected to this new kind of threat to knowledge: New television channels, magazines, and radio stations are being opened, especially aimed at younger people, trying to fill them with new thoughts and opinions related to issues which ultimately revolve around commercial interests. In such a climate, how are we to judge a new report on 'Arab Human Development' that does not utter a single word about the influence of commercial interests in corrupting knowledge or in impeding its progress?

–3–

I would like to ask readers to cast their minds back seventy years to when the famous Egyptian writer Taha Husayn wrote his important book, *The Future of Culture in Egypt*, in which he discusses exactly the same issue as that discussed in the UNDP report on 'The Knowledge Society.' Husayn's book was written in his name only, and he bore the sole responsibility for its contents and enjoyed complete freedom in what he would and would not say and how he would say it. He had no other motivation for writing it than his own and no international development organization asked him to write it. When he wrote a page, he knew that it would appear in the book exactly as he wrote it and not as part of a background paper to be reviewed by the head of a core team which would decide what would remain, what would be excised, and what would be modified. The writer was not simply a man of letters, he was also a thinker whose positions on public issues were well known. He took positions which were often controversial, but at least they were always made clear and he did not hide behind obscure expressions— that were obscure either because they were translated from a foreign language or because the work relied for its success partly upon the obscurity of its expressions.

How the world has changed in the past seven decades! Now the responsibility for the state of culture, education, and knowledge in Arab countries has been transferred to an organization with a name that is itself obscure, the United Nations Development Programme, and whose goals have been determined by people from outside the Arab world. A core team recruited Arab writers of differing opinions, from the left and the right, some strong supporters of the American invasion of Iraq while others are strong opponents of it, some low-key academicians while others are political activists, some enormously angry at Israeli actions in Palestine, while others are in favor of reconciliation, some with wide interests while others are narrowly specialized. They were all charged with writing what are called 'background papers,' on delivery of which their duties would come to an end. But in return, they were relieved of any responsibility for what the report would come out with in the end.

What sort of report could be produced under such an arrangement? The answer is: a report exactly of this kind. The sole position it takes may only be read between the lines, and the only conclusion to be drawn from it comes more from what it is silent about than from what it actually says.

The *Arab Human Development Report* does not make sufficient distinction between the performance of one Arab country and another, apparently hoping that bad performance will outweigh the good. Sufficient distinction is also not made between one era and another, apparently in the hope that what went on during a particularly bad time might cover up what the Arabs might do under better conditions. In any case, reference to any pressure from the outside, either from foreign countries or international organizations, is proscribed. In the words of the report "Exaggerating the impediments to Arab development imposed by regional and international challenges is futile and self-defeating. This all-too frequent resort may provide a comforting escape, yet it is still highly unproductive."[13]

In short, the *Arab Human Development Report* blocks any avenue of escape for the Arabs, while it piles on one criticism after another. For example, an earlier report published in the previous year,[14] compares the gross national product of Arab countries with that of Spain and finds that the GNP of the twenty-two Arab states is less than that of just that one state. The figures are correct, but to offer them without any explanation or clarification, and to place them alongside all of the other criticisms of Arab deficiencies, is nothing but an act of humiliation. The result was that no one who cares to bash the Arabs either in the West or from within the Arab world has failed to cite this comparison, not forgetting to remind the readers that those who wrote it are prominent figures from the Arab world itself writing for an international organization.

The writers of the report found the example of Spain particularly convenient because Spain is not usually regarded as one of the 'advanced countries.' Thus, its advancement beyond twenty-two Arab countries put together must show the Arabs in a particularly bad light. Nevertheless, this unflattering impression contains within itself a large red herring. Seven of the Arab states cited together comprise less than half the population of Spain. What is more, a slight increase in the price of oil could change these figures overnight in favor of the Arabs. The figures are cited to show that there is something seriously wrong with the Arabs that would permit a single country like Spain to surpass them all, but the same thing can be said with even greater resonance about a country like India. Spain, whose population is not more than forty million, has a larger gross national product than India, whose population is twenty-five times as large. Fortunately for India, however, the UNDP is not concerned just now with denouncing it but prefers for the time being to concentrate on the Arabs.

This objectionable way of using numbers continues in the 2003 report right from the first page. In the first paragraph of the introduction, we read the following:

> Last year's inaugural *Arab Human Development Report* was by any standard a phenomenon . . . as the more than one million copies downloaded off the Internet so far testifies. . . . *Time* magazine cited it as the most important publication of 2002. . . . The United Nations Development Programme is proud to have sponsored it.

Note what this sentence gives as a proof of the greatness of the first report, the number of times it was downloaded from the Internet and the statement in *Time* magazine. Anyone interested in the state of knowledge must surely know that the number of readers of a magazine, newspaper, or book is not a particularly good measure of its quality and not a sufficient reason for pride in that particular publication. We all know of newspapers in the United States and Europe whose circulation runs into the millions, but also of other magazines and books of much better quality whose readership is not more than a few thousand. Many of the papers with wide circulation depend upon scandal mongering or crime reports. When *Time* says that the report is the most important publication of 2002, this may seem innocent enough, but it just happens that, for some reason or another, this segment of the news media in the United States seems particularly keen on depicting the Arabs in the worst possible light. Nor could it be a sheer coincidence that the American Secretary of Defense, and indeed President Bush himself, used the report as one of the justifications for invading Iraq. When the situation reaches the level of the endorsement of the report by a magazine of such wide circulation as well as by such important personalities, it is no wonder that the report was downloaded a million times.

This is merely one but by no means the only misuse of numbers in the report. There is a common but mistaken perception that things that can be measured in numbers are more important than those that cannot, that the number of people convinced of a particular point of view is an indication of the veracity of that view, and that any slight variation in numbers is meaningful. The report adopts all of these mistaken perceptions and others, on one page after another, leaving its readers utterly exhausted and ready to accept any notion that follows from the stated figures. For example, the writers of the report express their dismay that the number of newspapers in Arab countries is fewer than fifty-three for every thousand people as compared with 275 per thousand in the advanced countries. They are also dismayed that the number of telephone lines is one-fifth of those in advanced countries, that the number of computers is eighteen per thousand in the Arab region as compared with the world average of 78.3 per thousand, and that the number of Internet users in the Arab world is limited to only 1.6 percent of the population. The average number of books translated per one million people in the Arab world in the first five years of the 1990s was 4.4 (which is less than one book per year for every million people), while the corresponding number was 519 books per million in Hungary and 920 per million in Spain.

The report is full of such numbers and comparisons. But here is another way of misusing numbers. The report team took a survey of faculty members at Arab universities about their opinion of the state of knowledge in their countries, the result of which is summarized as follows: "In general, respondents expressed their dissatisfaction with the state of knowledge acquisition in their countries (average level of satisfaction: 38 percent)." Indeed, their satisfaction with "the extent that knowledge acquisition serves human development was slightly smaller (average level: 35 percent)." The report sums the topic up by noting the "impression of a huge need for spurring the acquisition of knowledge in Arab countries."

What is the real significance of such figures, comparisons, and solicited opinions? Apart from the statistical objections one can make to the way these numbers are being read, what exactly is so wonderful about an increase in the numbers of people reading newspapers, translating books, or using the telephone? None of these is a measure of anything but itself. As for human progress, it surely is best measured using other means, if it can be measured at all.

Do the report writers favor a person who reads one or two papers every day to someone who prefers to spend the same amount of time talking to his neighbor, colleague, or family members? And how can we measure progress in terms of the consumption of daily newspapers without also considering whether those papers are of the quality, say, of the English paper the *Daily Mirror*, or the *Independent*, or the *Guardian*? Suppose the circulation of a paper like the *Daily Mirror* increases against the other two while the number of newspapers in the Arab world remains the same. In the view of the report writers, this would mean a relative deterioration in the "state of knowledge" in the Arab countries, inviting real alarm or maybe even a military invasion! True, there are countries that are more advanced than we are in many important things, but these things surely do not include the number of newspapers printed or the number of hours spent on the telephone.

The number of books translated needs a little more reflection. Readers might ask whether it refers to the number of books translated from Arabic into a foreign language or the other way round. But of course it must be the other way round for the writers must believe that it is the Arabs who need the translation and not any other nation, even with regard to literary works. The reason is that if other nations are more advanced than we are in science, they must also be more advanced in literature. But what then are the foreign languages they have in mind? They must mean English, French, or German and not Japanese, Chinese, or Korean. It is probably only the first group, in their view, that should be translated whether the books are books of science or literature. Let us, however, assume that they mean the translation of *any* language into Arabic. Should we still not reflect on the type of books translated? Should we also include detective stories and romance novels, regardless of how useful they may be, on the assumption that the translation of any book is always worthwhile?

The report goes on to compare the rate of translation in Arab countries with that in two other countries: Hungary and Spain. Those are both European nations, with the same cultural roots and belonging to the same civilization as other European countries. But Hungarian and Spanish readers may find novels, stories, and poems, even history, coming from other European countries more animating than Arab readers would. It may indeed be useful for some science books to be translated, but this still does not mean that the number of books per million people translated in Hungary or Spain should be the ideal number for the Arab world. The ideal number surely depends on a number of factors including, for example, whether a subject is studied in a foreign language or in the mother tongue. If Hungarian and Spanish students study medicine or engineering in their mother tongues while Arab students study them in English or French, then the need for translation is obviously greater for them in these subjects than it is for Arab students. The same observation holds when Spanish or Hungarian students are less willing for any reason to read textbooks in foreign languages than are Arab students.

One fundamental factor behind the low number of books translated in the Arab world is economic. It has to do with the poverty of a given country as a whole and with the distribution of income. This does not just explain the difference in the number of translated books, it also explains many of the other differences noted in the report, such as the consumption of books and newspapers, or computer use. When we acknowledge this, we will realize that the real problem lies with poverty. It is a bit of a mystery, then, that the UNDP report does not give the same emphasis to poverty as it gives to other things like authoritarian rule and religious extremism.

In the appendix, the report offers an opinion poll of the views of some Arab intellectuals about the state of knowledge—complete with colorful charts and graphs. Once again, the authors of the report try to support their point of view concerning the poor state of knowledge in Arab countries with numbers, this time derived from questionnaires and opinion polls. Here they face enough statistical and conceptual difficulties to cause any social scientist worth his salt to abandon the whole sterile exercise. But the report writers do not want to lose this important means of casting an objective, scientific color onto what they are saying. The appendix begins with apologies for using the numbers they have obtained, saying, for example, that "the sample of opinions is not exactly a random sampling of Arab intellectuals," which allows making direct generalization of the 'Arab intellectual society,' and that, "the views of every one of them is surely subjective." However, the report goes on to say that "the value of individual opinion increases as intellectual capital increases; the opinions of faculty members at universities are given extra weight because they are involved in the formation of human capital by their work in higher education."[15]

The conclusion drawn from the statistics in this section is that the respondents to the questionnaire generally expressed dissatisfaction with the state of knowledge acquisition in their countries (average satisfaction: 38 percent), while satisfaction with what is called "the extent to which Arab knowledge serves human development" was slightly less (average 35 percent).

I must confess my bewilderment about a number of things in that short paragraph: What is meant exactly by "the state of knowledge acquisition?" Or by "the extent to which Arab of knowledge serves human development"?, and what is meant by the "degree of satisfaction"? Is 38 percent a low or high degree of satisfaction? What number would have caused the authors of the report to be pleased about the state of knowledge in the Arab world? And is there any significance in the three-point drop in satisfaction with "the service of the acquisition of knowledge to human development" from the "average degree of satisfaction with the condition of knowledge acquisition"? Again, suppose the faculty members at some American universities were asked about their degree of satisfaction over, say, the state of American television, and it was found that their rate of satisfaction was 38 percent, what might we derive from this about the state of American television and the extent to which it serves 'human development in American society?' Would we say that this is a good state of affairs or a bad one? Finally, I wonder what someone like Voltaire, at the height of the European age of Enlightenment, might have given as his degree of satisfaction with the state of knowledge acquisition in France at the time, and whether it would have differed from his degree of satisfaction with the extent to which the acquisition of knowledge 'served human development' in France?

–4–

When the scheme called the 'Greater Middle East Initiative' was announced for the first time, encapsulating in a general way what the United States wished to accomplish in the Arab world (and some countries surrounding it), it was surprising to find that its goals were the same as those of the *Arab Human Development Report*s of 2002 and 2003, those being democracy, freedom, respect for human rights, the promotion of the state of knowledge, the empowerment of women, as well as faster development, especially with greater reliance on the private sector.

Anyone meeting such a declaration of goals would find much irony in them. The greatest is that any colonialist invasion, whether old-style or a more recent variety, always covers its real goals with lofty slogans. The invasion of Iraq is unlikely to be different from earlier colonialist campaigns. Thus, the use of the slogans of democracy, greater knowledge, the empowerment of women, and faster development could very well be mere façades for other goals, such as the control of oil, opening markets, or the greater empowerment of Israel.

Then suddenly came the news about what the occupation forces were doing in a prison at Abu Ghraib, when the startling pictures showing the way Iraqi prisoners were treated were broadcast around the world, some showing horribly original forms of torture. Many of these prisoners were not arrested for anything they had done, but merely for what it was feared they might do or on the slightest suspicion that they might have done. When reflecting upon the photos, what was written about them, and the statements of American officials, including the Secretary of Defense and the President himself, I found that it all shed stark light on the meaning of 'human development' as it is understood by the authors of the Greater Middle East Initiative.

———

Let us first take democracy, liberty, and human rights. Abu Ghraib revealed a strange understanding of these glorious slogans. According to this understanding, democracy does not prevent thousands of Iraqis from being thrown into prison on the merest suspicion, or even by pure happenstance, without any charge leveled against them. One of the prisoners in Abu Ghraib was an Iraqi man who had stolen a toothbrush; another had been riding a bus to Baghdad to get a license of some sort, when the bus was stopped and searched, and he was arrested for no reason. Yet another was a woman who had heard some odd noises and stepped out of her house to see what they were; it turned out to be the American soldiers raiding a neighbor's house, and when she stepped out to see, she was arrested along with everyone else. The way they were treated in Abu Ghraib prison was shown in the pictures: piles of Iraqi bodies with a couple of American soldiers standing behind them grinning, or an American girl dragging a naked Iraqi man along the floor of the prison by a dog leash.

When President Bush was asked about the pictures, he expressed his sorrow, but he did not apologize. When in a press conference at the White House the editor of the Egyptian newspaper *al-Ahram* pressed him politely about the pictures and whether they warranted an apology from him, President Bush again expressed his sorrow but did not apologize.

Many things were said to lessen the impact of Abu Ghriab. It was said that Abu Ghraib was an isolated incident, not a general phenomenon. It was pointed out that President Bush expressed not only his sorrow but even his disgust at what had happened, that this was also the feeling of all Americans, and that the torture in no way represented the feelings of Americans toward Arabs. The British Foreign Secretary said that we must not exaggerate the significance of what had happened and that we must not forget the Americans and British who had been killed by Iraqis. It was said also that we should not forget what Saddam Hussein had been doing to his people before the occupation and, indeed, the way many Arab governments torture and humiliate their own people in no less horrible ways. Some commentators pointed out that the wide publication of the photos in the American media, which led to the questioning of the Secretary of Defense by Congress, was an indication of the transparency of the American political system: the truth cannot be hidden from the people; crimes do not go unpunished; and wrong doing is nipped in the bud. This is exactly what the rest of the world should be imitating and what the Arabs in particular are lacking.

The depiction of Abu Ghraib as an isolated incident may be taken to mean that it was the result of the action of some deranged man or woman with sadistic tendencies, who enjoyed visions of torture and of men being dragged along a prison floor like dogs. But the details of the photos themselves show how things proceeded. The torture was carried out in wide hallways and open prison yards with soldiers and officers coming and going. In one picture, a young woman poses smoking a cigarette and grinning for the camera while flashing the victory sign with one hand and pointing at a pile of naked bodies with the other. In another, she and an older male colleague pose smiling. The piling of one naked Iraqi upon another is not something a single man or woman can accomplish but requires the cooperation of many and could never happen without the knowledge of some authority. The shipping, preparation, and use of the wires, batons, and other devices employed in the torture also require the cooperation of many people, perhaps even as far away as the United States. When the names of the men and women involved were published in the papers, it was never said, as far as I know, that any one of them was mentally deficient or suffering from any treatable psychological condition that would compel them to engage in such acts. What is more credible is that those committing the crimes and their superiors, just like thousands of other Americans over many years, and especially since the events of September 11, have succumbed to the besmirching of Arabs in the American media, depicting the Arabs in ways that suggest that the Arabs deserve no better treatment than they got at Abu Ghraib. This climate is still being perpetuated by the American media, from Hollywood films to the books of Bernard Lewis. The torture does not indeed look like an isolated phenomenon but rather like a reflection of a general mood expressed, not just in Abu Ghraib but also and increasingly in American and European mass media.

But regardless of how outraged we were about American behavior at Abu Ghraib, we must admit that it does not provide any room to doubt American advancement in many things addressed by the UNDP reports on Arab human development of the last few years. In those same things, Arabs are far behind, whether with regard to the empowerment of women, the achievement of a knowledge society, or the rapid progress in private sector-driven development.

Where the empowerment of women is concerned, the most important personalities in the pictures and reports about Abu Ghraib were two women. The first is Janet Karpinski, who rose through the ranks of the army, finally becoming a general and the commandant of Abu Gharib. The second is a young woman no older than twenty-one years of age by the name of Lyndie England, who grew up in a poor area of West Virginia, one of the poorest states in America, and who had been married and divorced before she finished her schooling. She joined the United States army as a means of getting to college, and she had a relationship with one of her colleagues in Abu Ghraib, Charles Grand, by whom she became pregnant. She is the girl who appeared in one of the pictures laughing and smoking a cigarette while flashing the victory sign and pointing at the private parts of a hooded Iraqi. She also appeared in another photo dragging another naked Iraqi by a leash.

Pictures like this would not have been familiar (maybe not even imaginable) forty or fifty years ago. Western society has undoubtedly achieved great progress during that time, not just in photographic technology and the art of torture, but also in the empowerment of women. As a result of the great progress achieved by American women (and women in the West in general) in the last fifty years, wider work opportunities have opened up for them and their wages have risen, which has allowed them to play a larger role in public life. Added to all this is the way women have become like men: in their clothing, as may be seen in Lyndie's style of dress in the pictures; in their way of cutting their hair (as may also be seen in the photos); and in the fact that they can now join the army as enlisted soldiers and officers on the same footing as men. This had to lead to women taking part in torture in the same way men do. As long as women are proving that they can shoulder physical and psychological burdens to the same degree as men, they also should be able, it seems, to torture Iraqis without undergoing a feeling of shame.

Any talk now about the biological or psychological differences between men and women that would compel them to behave differently must appear foolish and open to debate after what we have seen and heard about Abu Ghraib. What greater strength might we ask of women now than that they be able to drag a naked Iraqi man like a dog along the floor of a prison? What depravity might we be able to allege that men are more capable of committing compared with women?

This, then, must be one of the things we wish the Arabs to achieve in the field of the empowerment of women and the lifting of their oppression. Here we have Western women not only escaping the oppression of men but also able to oppress men.

As for the 'knowledge society,' it seems to include the use of advanced interrogation devices for extracting confessions attached to various parts of the prisoners' bodies. Meters track their physical responses on computer screens so that prisoners will not die before their interrogators decide that they should. Of course, none of these devices and torture techniques for obtaining the best results from prisoners could have been achieved without great progress in biological and behavioral sciences. The broadcast of what was happening in Abu Ghraib was itself achieved by means made available by the information and communications revolution, beginning with the great clarity of the photos, taken in poor light, and then the ability to broadcast them all over the world through various media as soon as their existence became known. The sheer repetition with which a single picture or news item can reach an audience throughout the day, also made possible by the information and communication revolutions, adds to the effect, aside from the way it can be dispersed to millions or billions of people.

It may be said that this quality of information dispersal may not be effective at all, as people become inured to sights of torture and humiliation, and the information loses the psychological impact it may once have had. On the other hand, the repeated appearance of people belonging to a particular nation or members of a particular religion in scenes of torture, beatings, and hatred could sully their image in perpetuity and render people more ready to insult and hate them. But what is the import of all this compared with the ability to disperse knowledge to all, or the ability of people in all parts of the world to see color pictures of events in their living rooms within a few minutes of their happening, and with no more effort than the press of a button? The important thing seems to be the sheer amount of information and the number of people it reaches. The content, utility, or even the truth of the information seems to be of little importance in the measure of progress.

Finally, we come to privatization or development through the private sector. Abu Ghraib seems also to have become an important laboratory for encouraging the private sector to enter new fields that had formerly been the reserve of governments or the public sector. I mean particularly the field of torture. The United States Department of Defense must have considered it useful and more efficient not to place interrogation and torture operations solely in the hands of the men and women of the Department, who are after all government employees. The American philosophy considers a public employee to be necessarily less efficient than any worker in private (or free) enterprise. The public employee will not budge except in the public interest, and such motivation is weak and unreliable, whereas people by nature only act in self-interest or when moved by the profit motive. It appears that what applies to the economic sphere also applies to torture. Torture would also be more efficient if it were conducted under the profit motive. Imagine, for example, American soldiers or officers, who draw their paychecks from the Defense Department, interrogating a prisoner about the names and addresses of his colleagues taking part in the resistance to the American occupation. Their paychecks are not affected whether they obtain a confession or not. Indeed, their resolve may be weakened a bit by pity for some of those being tortured for no good reason. True, they may receive a commendation from their superiors if they do manage to obtain a confession, but how do they compare with someone working for a private company hired by the Defense Department to interrogate and torture Iraqis for the same ends? Such a person knows full well that the size of his dollar income depends upon his success in obtaining con-fessions. His efficiency may presumably be reckoned in the number of confessions he can extract, the number of heads he bashes, or the number of bodies he interrogates (that is, tortures). Aside from that, he faces no punishment if he uses torture methods that cross the line of humanity, and is not restrained by the legal sanctions imposed on public employees if they overstep their authority. The private sec-tor employee is only governed by the terms of his contract. The worst thing that could be imposed upon him is to have his contract revoked and that he be sent home.

Here you see the extent of efficiency realized by reliance upon the private sector even in torture, where the greatest benefit is obtained at the lowest expense. It admits no humanitarian and ethical considerations or any other such silly things in pursuit of the desired result.

This then, is the model of 'human development' when realized in the style of Abu Ghraib, whether with regard to democracy, respect for human rights, transparency, greater empowerment of women, wider dispersal of knowledge, or the opening of the broadest avenue for the private sector, even in the most personal of human affairs. These are some of the things that the Arabs are badly in need of learning from the advanced countries of the West.

4

Freedom

In 1999 a book was published that met many of the conditions of success, but a success which is not necessarily of the best kind. The author is a prominent economist who has been active since the 1950s, first as a lecturer and then as a professor at the prestigious British university of Cambridge. During his time there, he published many books that successfully combined economics, politics, philosophy, and ethics, and his books were well received by economists, especially those working in the fields of development and economic welfare. After years of teaching at Cambridge, the author moved on to two other prestigious British universities, the University of London and then Oxford. He was also a visiting professor at Harvard, the Massachusetts Institute of Technology, Berkeley, and Stanford in the United States. He and a prominent Pakistani economist, Mahbub ul-Haq, cooperated in the formulation of the concept of human development which was adopted by the United Nations and an office by that name was founded and attached to the U.N. Development Programme. Crowning all this was his being awarded the Nobel Prize in Economics in 1998. He is the Indian economist Amartya Sen, and the book we are concerned with is his *Development as Freedom*.[16]

A renowned professor, an important subject, a catchy title, and the Nobel Prize; this should guarantee the success of the book. Despite all that, the more I read of his book, the more uncomfortable I felt, a discomfort that sometimes verged on irritation and even anger. Let me now explain why.

Human beings have numerous needs and desires. Economists may be exaggerating when they assert that these needs and desires are unlimited, but they are indeed numerous. There are material and non-material needs, from food, clothing, and shelter to transportation, human communication, and forming social bonds. If these are all things that people cannot do without, there are also many desires people aspire to that are not necessities in that sense. People want many forms of entertainment, leisure time, and things that bring them prestige or power. They may want to be able to express their inner selves with some form of artistic expression, and they want reassurance from all sorts of fears, such as the fear of losing a loved one, the fear of poverty, of unemployment, of loneliness, and of course, of death.

Human needs may be relatively fixed, but there are many desires that are always changing and may vary greatly from one society to another. The desires of the members of a small society are not the same as those of citizens of a large state, and the wants of villagers are not the same as those of city-dwellers. Those of nomads are not the same as those of sedentary agriculturalists or of urbanites in an industrial society. But even if needs and wants were fixed and shared among all people, they may still vary from one individual to another according to preference or inclination and with differences in mental and physical ability, sex, religion, and so on.

But if human needs and desires are many and varied to such a degree, the restrictions that may be put on them that could prevent people from fulfilling them must also be many and varied. Poverty can restrict or prevent the fulfilling of needs; bad health can prevent people from doing much of what they may wish to do; and ignorance or lack of information can prevent people from reaching their goals if reaching them requires possessing a minimum amount of information. The despotism practiced by one person against others may prevent them from realizing their needs or satisfying their desires. But despotism itself comes in many guises and has many possible sources; it may arise in the dealings of a state with its people, in the relationship between men and women, in the behavior of a father lording over his children, or of a manager of a corporation over his employees. It can come from religious institutions and may even originate in social customs and traditions that cause people to have a feeling of guilt if they pursue certain desires. Not to mention terrorism, about which a lot, indeed too much, is being said lately.

We should note also that the very agents that may prevent people from satisfying some of their needs or desires may also, and at the same time, be the means for meeting other needs. A state might prohibit citizens from traveling outside its borders, but it may simultaneously provide guaranteed employment, for instance, or protection against terrorism. Prevalent traditions may instill feelings of shame in people for gratifying certain desires, but they may also oblige others to care for those same people when they grow old. Other traditions may work in exactly the opposite fashion; that is, they may free people from feelings of shame for committing certain acts, but they may not guarantee the fulfillment of other needs or desires.

There is of course nothing new in saying all this. What *is* somewhat new is Sen's manner of expressing it, and that exactly is what propelled me to begin addressing the matter in a somewhat different manner. In *Development as Freedom*, Sen chooses to speak of all these needs and desires by employing the concept of freedom. He describes human needs and desires as if they are all synonyms for the desire for freedom. Satisfying the need for food becomes in his estimation freedom to eat or not to eat when hungry. Likewise the need for clothing, shelter, information, or movement; all of these are transformed into the freedom to acquire this or that or not to acquire it, or into the freedom to perform or not to perform a certain act. If this is the case, then all obstacles or impediments to meeting needs or fulfilling desires can be referred to as 'restrictions on freedom.' Poverty is a restriction on the freedom to obtain many of the necessities of life; bad health becomes a restriction on the freedom to live a healthy life; and ignorance or the lack of opportunity to go to school or university becomes a restriction on the freedom to acquire knowledge. The same can be said for the autocracy of the state, the imposition by certain religious institutions of their own interpretations of religion on people, the weight of custom and tradition, male dominance over women, the tyranny of fathers over their children, and so on.

This route chosen by Sen may at first glance seem harmless; it may even appear attractive. There is, of course, an attraction in attributing many things to the same cause, in this case, freedom, in addition to the attraction of the concept of freedom itself. Viewing the fulfillment of various needs and desires as the realization of the lofty goal of freedom inflates the value of those needs and increases the significance of any form of deprivation of needs and desires. This presentation of the problem has many shortcomings, however. For what exactly is the advantage to our viewing poverty, bad health, single-party rule, the effect of a certain tradition or culture with regard to keeping women out of work, state intervention in the marketplace, and forcing new graduates into certain jobs, as if they were all merely different manifestations of one particular phenomenon: the loss of freedom? Could this be simply a play on words that may conceal more than it reveals?

Sure, in poverty there is a restriction of freedom of one sort or another, just as there is in the imposition of price controls. Nevertheless, are there not enormous differences between those two phenomena presented merely as two forms of a loss of freedom? There is, in the first place, a difference in the degree of suffering involved. In the case of poverty, the loss of freedom may reach the point of being unable to choose between life and death, if people are forced to die of hunger, or to choose between enjoying the feeling of personal dignity and being humiliated by others. In the case of price controls, however, the loss of freedom involves hardly more than the loss of the producer's ability to fix the price of his goods or to move into more profitable activities. Indeed, the loss of freedom to some caused by price controls may be smaller than the gain of freedom realized by others, those being the poorer consumers who were denied those goods before the price control. The loss of freedom that attends poverty is certainly much more oppressive than that felt by those prohibited from changing certain amounts of their national currency into foreign currency. Thus talking about these different types of deprivation or failure to meet needs or desires as if they were merely different examples of the same thing, that is, deprivation of freedom, may do more harm than good.

There is also some harm in settling an issue over which a controversy still rages, that is, to depict the problem in all of these cases as if it always revolves around disagreement between proponents of freedom and its enemies. All of us may be ready to concede that freedom is something that is always to be desired, a worthwhile goal under any circumstances. It is easy, however, to fall into the trap of thinking that the problem can be solved simply by taking the side of freedom against its enemies, when the problem is much more complex and the solution much more difficult to find.

Take, for example, Sen's discussion of the dispute between advocates of a free market system and advocates of state intervention in a chapter entitled 'Markets, State, and Social Opportunity.' The author admits that the state should under certain circumstances intervene to insure greater justice by producing what economists call 'public goods,' namely goods and services that may bring no profit to any particular person or group of people but benefit the society as a whole—things like education, defense, healthcare, or public parks, which may not be produced at all if we rely upon the profit motive alone. But the thing on which he puts the greatest emphasis, and the basic message he makes sure that the reader takes away, is that a free market system, or the absence of government intervention in the choices that individuals make about production and consumption, is the best system. He justifies this argument not only by the usual defense of the market system, namely that it achieves the greatest level of efficiency, but also on the ground that the market system leaves people free in conducting their business. The market system, in Sen's view, has therefore another benefit aside from that of efficiency, that is, it achieves the lofty goal of freedom.

Presented in this way the issue seems to have been decided in favor of the market. The truth is, however, that it is far from being settled. The claim that the market system is the most efficient system is controversial, especially if we understand the word 'efficient' to include ethical and aesthetic considerations in addition to purely material and quantifiable benefits and also to include the interests of future generations, all of which could justify a large intervention by the state. But apart from this, the contribution of the market in increasing freedom is itself a doubtful matter that requires more careful deliberation. Leaving people free to take their own decisions without any interference from the state seems at first glance to allow people greater freedom compared with a system that subjects them to restrictions and commands. Nevertheless, people, if allowed to take decisions freely, may very well produce in the end a less 'free' society than a system of restrictions and commands.

It may be said that this is what Sen means by allowing state intervention to insure equity. The term 'equity,' however, if taken to mean protection of the weak against the aggression of the strong, is a much broader term than Sen portrays it to be in this book and than readers might imagine it to be. With every step we take, we may find a situation that could call for some intervention on behalf of the weak and in which leaving people free without any regulation reduces the amount of freedom available to some but not to others. The issue is not merely that of protecting consumers and labor from the depredations of monopolies, or of state provision of basic education to people who might not get it if it were left to profit-seeking enterprises. The assault of advertisements and hawkers of goods in the mass media, for example, encouraging a consumerist lifestyle, which the market system necessarily elicits, could suppress freedom in no less dangerous a fashion than powerful state intervention. The point is that the market system while giving some freedom with one hand may take other freedoms away with the other. Thus the claim that the market system is necessarily more able to provide freedom to people than is a system of state intervention is far too hasty.

Professor Sen also raises the issue of freedom while discussing problems involved in the encounters between cultures and civilizations. Here Sen admits that the subject is fraught with peril. He expresses some sympathy with the view of those who fear the invasion by Western culture of their national cultures and he sees the parallel between the possible results of this invasion and the danger of extinction to which some animals are subject. But the main message that readers take away from this chapter is that there is no serious danger and that there are no real grounds for worry. In the first place, civilizations and cultures are always interacting, such that it is very rare to find any instances of a pure culture with no traces of influence from other cultures. All the values that we take pride in, like tolerance and democracy, are present to some degree in many cultures, such as the Hindu or Islamic. India invaded the West with its culture just as Western culture invaded India (his example of the Indian invasion of the West, however, is the appearance of the plates of chicken masala in British restaurants), and the things with which the West has invaded India are often originally Indian goods returning back to India. So what is there to complain about?

But here is another message that the author wishes to convey in this chapter: namely that the solution to these issues, just as it is with most issues raised in other chapters of the book, is to grant people the freedom of choice. The various cultures of the Third World are now being offered the choice between Western culture and their own, and all that is being asked of them is to choose what they regard as the best, or, in other words to assess cultural products the way economists assess projects and to choose the one with the greatest net benefits.

Here Sen is obviously ignoring the fact that the competition between cultures is far from being a fair one, with the odds heavily in favor of one against the others. The chance of success of this one culture in obliterating the others stems not necessarily from its moral or aesthetic superiority but from its superior economic, political, and military power, and hence the supposed 'freedom of choice' is often severely lacking.

Sen's discussion of women's issues led him to similar conclusions. According to Sen, women in the Third World are oppressed and subject to many types of discrimination. He argues that apart from the obvious fact that such treatment of women constitutes an important denial of freedom, a greater empowerment of women would bring about additional benefits such as lowering the fertility rate and raising the level of health care and of education for children, especially for girls; indeed it could play an important role in supporting general economic, political, and social progress, along with protecting the environment. According to Sen, there is evidence to show that when women are entrusted with such things they are no less efficient at undertaking them than are men. To support this view, Sen brings up statistics from some Indian states showing that when the percentage of women increases against men, the percentage of violent crime decreases.

We do not wish to question the significance of these statistics; there are good logical reasons to endorse the use which Sen makes of them, even if they may not be conclusive. The important thing to notice however is that all of the examples of the oppression of and discrimination against women adduced by Sen come from the Third World. This would cause the reader to come away with the impression that women's problems have been completely solved or nearly so in the Western industrialized world. Many could argue, however, that the greater economic liberation of women and the lifting of many forms of oppression and discrimination against them in the way the West has been doing for the last hundred years—and with regard to which the Third World has not made much progress—has been accompanied by, and has even created other forms of oppression and restrictions of freedom not mentioned by Sen. I am thinking of the oppression faced by Western women at the hands of growing commercialism, the emergence of the consumer society, and the increasing use of women as sex symbols. I am also thinking of the oppression women face from the break-up of the family that has been occurring as women achieve greater economic independence, and indeed probably as a direct result of that economic independence. I am not saying which situation is better, nor could one belittle the gains that women have made in economic freedom, I am only pointing out that the situation may not be as simple as Sen suggests.

What should have worried Sen more than it apparently did is that women's gain in the sphere of freedom has not been associated merely with losses of a different kind, but actually with losses in the sphere of freedom itself. The mother who for one reason or another is obliged to raise her children alone because of the break-up of the family is freer than others in some respects, but she is less free in other ways, as for instance when she is forced to accept a job that she would not have accepted otherwise. By bringing up the subject of the break-up of the family and the weakening of family ties, we are therefore not moving away from the subject of freedom so dear to Professor Sen's heart.

What happened seems to be something like this: Professor Sen looked around and found the whole world talking about freedom, democracy, and the triumph of the market system, about globalization and the transformation of the world into a global village, as well as about the greater empowerment of women. By writing a book that reduces every thing to freedom or the lack of it, a writer could kill many birds with one stone: he could praise democracy, the market system, globalization, and defend women while at the same time showing the Third World that there is really no trade off between the noble goal of development and other noble goals. All goals were being poured into one vessel: freedom. In this way the world would look quite beautiful, or at least it would look as if despite the existence of a few unlovely things it was headed in the right direction in all of these areas—politics, the economy, social relations, and even international and intercultural relations between the developed and the less-developed world.

There is, then, nothing for the less-developed world to fear from the more developed one, neither for the economy, nor for politics, nor even for its cultures. Globalization is not only inevitable, but is also, in the final analysis, for the good of all, on the condition that some minor interventions are made in the interest of the 'marginalized,' and also on the condition that the people of the poorer parts of the world exercise their freedom of choice between the various cultures being presented to them. It is, after all, nothing different from the age-old interactions between different cultures. The picture Sen paints of the world in his book is certainly a pretty one: we have no reason to be angry, the enemies of globalization have no right to resist it, those who oppose the market system really have no serious grounds for criticizing it, and those who love their culture have no good reason to rebuff the Western cultural invasion or to fall into despair. True, there is a need for a bit of retouching here and there, but the picture is basically wonderful; anyway, it is not likely to become much more wonderful than it is.

5

Democracy

We live in an era which boasts of the flowering of democracy. But what if the opposite is true, namely that we live in an era whose salient characteristic is the weakness that has overtaken the democratic system, even in the oldest countries in the history of democracy?

We need not be surprised if the rhetoric is directly opposed to the facts, for this is by no means the only example. Our epoch also boasts of being the epoch of economic development, or even of human development and respect for human rights, when it is closer to being an era in which various cultures are being oppressed by one dominant culture. The transfer of capital from rich to poor countries for a variety of selfish reasons has been referred to as economic aid, while an aggressive attitude by a group of countries toward much weaker ones is referred to as a clash of civilizations.

What is surprising is the readiness of a large number of people to close their eyes to glaring indications of the decline of democracy and to the weakness that has afflicted the party system, where it has become increasingly difficult to distinguish one political party from another, and where winning or losing an election increasingly depends on the personality of the leader of the party or of the candidate for president.

Notice also the deterioration in the level of political debate in the media, with politicians relying on their abilities to rouse people's emotions in their speeches and pronouncements more than on the strength of their arguments or the soundness of their logic. Indeed, look at the change that has come over politicians' and party leaders' personal qualities, how they have come close to being public relations men, distinguishable by their public appeal and personal attractions rather than by their convictions or their probity and ideological backgrounds. Then look at the increase in the number of corruption cases among politicians, which indicates their increasing readiness to surrender to the temptation to use their positions for material gain by facilitating transactions for business and living off the monetary support of businessmen in return for advancing their political interests.

All of these developments strike at the core of democracy. After all, one of the main measures of democracy is the influence which the average person can exercise in political decisions simply by virtue of being a citizen, regardless of race, gender, social class, wealth, or education. This requires that a citizen has the right to stand for parliament and to vote for candidates without any obstruction arising from his origin or from any of the factors mentioned above, or from any attempt at corrupting his or her choice.

But many of the developments that have occurred in political life, to which I have just referred, have led to increasing discrimination, giving some persons unjustified weight in the taking of decisions and corrupting the process of choice, either through the suppression of the information necessary for making the right choices, by distorting available information, or through the manipulation of the peoples' will, leading them in directions that are often opposed to their interest.

To forge election results is only one form of this distortion of the peoples' will, and a very primitive one at that, as well as the easiest to detect. And because it is so primitive and easy to detect it is also less dangerous than other ways of corrupting democracy. Everyone knows that the Soviet regime or the Nazis were not democratic, and everyone knows that most Third World regimes that call themselves democratic are not. But few people are ready to admit that a serious decline has overtaken democracy even in the states that were ahead of others in building democratic institutions.

Doubtless, one of the things that has underpinned this refusal to admit the decline of democracy is our persistence in the belief that human society generally and continuously marches from bad to better, and the belief that the most economically and technologically advanced societies are also, by necessity, the most advanced in their social and political organization.

Democratic development in the industrialized countries during the twentieth century was closely associated with the growth of power of trade union movements, which itself was associated with the growth of the size of industrial enterprises, allowing greater concentration of labor in one place and the growth of the share of industrial labor in the total labor force. Industrial laborers are for a number of reasons more capable of practicing political pressure than those engaged in agriculture and thus their growing strength during the first half of the century led to a more active political life and gave greater force to the process of greater democratization. An important change seems to have occurred, however, in the last quarter of the twentieth century when as a result mainly of technological developments the political power of labor unions started to decline, leading in turn to a weakening of the process.

This decline in the political power of industrial labor was partly the result of the decline of the share of industry in national output and of the reduction of the share of industrial labor in the total labor force to the advantage of those working in the service sector. Industrial labor also underwent a noticeable change in its structure to the advantage of higher-skilled workers and at the expense of manual and unskilled laborers. Service sector workers are on the whole less politicized and more dispersed and are thus less able to mount political action as a unified force than are industrial laborers. In addition, laborers with higher skills may feel that the gap that separates them from other industrial laborers is greater than the gap that exists between themselves and their employers, and their interests may not be identical with those of manual and unskilled workers. As such, they do not share a strong political bond with the other segments of labor. On top of this, and again as a response to technological developments, giant corporations in both manufacturing and service sectors tend to increase that share of their activities that is conducted on a global scale, shifting domestic jobs to foreign workers and transferring investment from one country to another, leading further to the weakening of the bargaining as well as the political power of industrial labor.

With the enhancement of the economic power of these giant corporations, their political influence was also enhanced, not just toward their workers but also toward politicians and policy makers. For these corporations are now able not only to threaten to move their investments elsewhere but also to overpower politicians and ruling coalitions and to force their will on them. We thus find ourselves before a new caste of the economically powerful who can just about debilitate any power that opposes them whether from below, coming from the workers, or from above, coming from those in positions of political power, whereas not much more than three decades ago, those two forces together were able effectively to limit the power of corporations.

In the light of the growth of the economic power of giant corporations, foreign as well as domestic policies have become, more than ever before, among the concerns of these corporations and an element in their strategic planning. True, politics have often reflected economic interests, but whereas it was possible fifty years ago for owners or managers of industrial enterprises to ignore foreign or domestic policies, as these had only a weak influence on their production and marketing strategies, politics can now rarely be ignored by big business. A man like Winston Churchill, for example, while minister of defense in the British government during the First World War, may indeed have had to pay close attention to the demands of captains of industry and British producers of armaments before he could make some of his major decisions. Nevertheless, we should expect that, with the great increase in the power of corporations over the last hundred years, the decisions taken by, say, the American secretary of defense at the turn of the twenty-first century would be much more in line with the wishes of the owners and managers of corporations and far less independent of them.

Part of this loss of independence is what is sometimes known as corruption, wherein the politician is beholden to the company he worked for before taking office or where he hopes to work when he leaves it. The increase in the number of such cases of corruption helps to explain the tipping of the balance of power between those with economic might and political decision-makers without our having to venture far afield into speculations about possible changes in the standards of morality or personal integrity. It also helps to explain the increase in the incidence of corruption in the political life of poorer countries without straying into a discussion of the moral standards of individuals in those countries either. It is quite enough to note the extent to which giant corporations have insinuated themselves among decision-makers in those countries, to the point of sometimes choosing them by name.

Also as a result of economic and technological developments, the interference of the economically powerful in the media has definitely increased. The owners and managers of giant corporations have greater need now to influence the media than at any time in the past, if only because the size of the markets they need to control is also greater than ever. At the same time, there has been an increase in the media's reliance on financing from such corporations. It is not surprising, then, that monopolies should develop in the world of mass media, with one company or even a single person taking ownership of a number of major newspapers while at the same time controlling several television channels. As a result, newspaper readers and television viewers tend to get more or less the same opinions repeated in different ways in newspapers and on television programs even though they may look superficially different. Little wonder that these corporations and individuals who control the media enjoy such great power and control over candidates for political office that their rise to the highest office or their fall from grace are at the mercy of any manner of boosterism and scandal-mongering.

In the light of these developments, why should one attach so much importance to the elections that come every few years, whether their results are forged or not? If major political parties look very much alike to the extent that they all flog a single program, or their differences largely disappear as soon as they take office, and if newspapers, or a least the important ones, and the major mass media outlets all say more or less the same thing even though in different ways, why should it matter whether voter registration is faked or real or whether vote counts are accurate?

There are indeed many indications that an increasing number of people are beginning to realize this, if with varying degrees of clarity. What is more, the percentage of voters taking part in elections, even in the oldest democracies, is declining. An increasing number of people are seeking alternatives to politics in areas where they are perhaps able to experience greater individual liberty, including sports, shopping, and entertainment. This decline of interest in politics is noticeably reflected in the amount of space and of airtime that the media dedicates to news and political commentary compared with the amount they dedicate to sports, entertainment, and various forms of consumption boosting.

It may be asked, have you not noticed that there are other developments that indicate a move in the other direction? Also as a result of technological and economic advances, opposition groups now have new media available to them for protest and for registering their opposition, for communicating with other people, and for organizing meetings, conferences, and demonstrations. The Internet is a new outlet that is an easy and cheap way of mobilizing an increasing number of people whose influence has been apparent in the growth of anti-globalization movements, for example, or of the opposition to the American and British occupation of Iraq and of the skepticism shown toward official pronouncements or those propagated by a press subservient to big business. Does not all of this indicate a healthy development toward greater political participation allowing people more equal opportunities in political decision-making regardless of their race, gender, or economic might?

It would be wrong, of course, to carry pessimism too far. In the long history of technological and economic development, one can easily detect two divergent trends: one toward greater liberation and the other toward greater oppression. To admit this, however, in no way justifies all that boasting about the flourishing of democracy. The development of new means of protest and contact among the dissidents merely raises a hope that one wishes would be fulfilled in the future. We should not shield our eyes from the startling development of forces working against it, that is, the suppression of voices of protest and the successful efforts made toward the diversion of people's attention away from politics.

6

Capitalism

About a century and a half ago, just when the capitalist system was showing great vigor and outstanding
success, Karl Marx and his colleague, Friedrich Engels, predicted the fall of capitalism. England and France had
completed their industrial revolutions, Germany and the
United States were on the verge of completing theirs, and
classical British economists were declaring with confidence
that this system based on individual incentives and competition for profit was the one to vouchsafe the wealth of
nations. The basic defect of the capitalist system, according to Marx and Engels, had to do with the distribution of
income and wealth. True, the capitalist system did lead to
an increase in the wealth of nations (even if it was characterized by cycles of rising and falling income), but the
system also engendered persistent and increasing poverty
alongside the increasing wealth. This unsatisfactory state
of affairs would, according to them, tend to accelerate until
it reached the point at which it blows up in the form of violent revolution led by the working class, and the explosion
would inevitably replace capitalism with socialism.

This logic led to the expectation of a socialist revolution
taking place first in the most advanced capitalist countries,

not in the most backward, as the most advanced capitalist country is obviously the one where the contradictions between wealth and poverty reach their greatest extent. What actually happened was that in 1917 a revolution erupted in one of the least developed capitalist countries, Russia, with its leaders claiming that it was the revolution predicted by Marx even though he had expected it to occur in Britain or in Germany. The Marxists themselves paid no heed to this and went on believing for more than seventy years that it was indeed the Russian Revolution that Marx had predicted. Some of them may still think that to this day, while opponents of Marxism consider this an indication of a grave error in their logic and of the devastating failure of Marx's predictions.

It is very possible, however, to argue that both sides were in error. The Russian Revolution was not the revolution to replace capitalism with socialism that Marx had predicted, but the critics of Marxism were also wrong in thinking that Marx was mistaken in predicting that disparities in the distribution of income must ultimately bring about a new system. True, the capitalist system did not fall in 1917, and socialism did not emerge as Marx had envisioned it, for the simple reason that such things do not really happen this way. Social systems do not fall as governments do as a result of a revolution or insurrection, and they do not change the way constitutions and laws do. Social systems change slowly and gradually. Developments may come about that cause them to be in the end something entirely different from what they were in the beginning, but this may happen without any revolution or insurrection, and people may continue to call them by their old names as if nothing had happened.

That is what seems to have occurred with capitalism during the century following the predictions made by Marx and Engels (1850–1950). Some important things did conform to what Marx had expected and some important things were contrary to his expectations, but this calls neither for great admiration nor for scorn. The great disparity between wealth and income did indeed increase, as Marx predicted, during the latter decades of the nineteenth century, and he was right when he said that it was impossible for the system to sustain a disparity between wealth and income beyond a certain point. He seems also to have been right in expecting that some kind of collective ownership would supersede individual ownership. He was wrong however in expecting the change to come in the form of a revolution; he never expected that the correction might occur by other, more peaceful and less clamorous means, or that collective ownership might not necessarily take the form of state ownership. He did not foresee that the scope of ownership could be expanded without confiscation or nationalization.

It turned out that such things can happen, and they have. Consider for instance the growth of joint stock companies. Are not these companies, owned by millions of small shareholders, a type of collective ownership that effects a sort of redistribution of wealth, with a capable manager (even if he is not an owner) filling the place of a large owner or a small number of owners? Consider also the capitalists having to bow to the demands of labor unions for better wages, shorter hours, and improved working conditions, permitting them more and more enjoyment of a much higher level of living. Or consider Keynesian policies that called for and led to greater intervention of the state to save Western countries from economic depression, or the welfare state that arose at the end of the Second World War, which redistributed income and provided essential services to all.

If classical economists were to have seen the state of the industrial world at mid-twentieth century—a century after the publication of John Stuart Mill's *Principles of Political Economy*, in which the essence of capitalist thought was presented, and of *The Communist Manifesto*, in which Marx and Engels predicted the fall of capitalism—how much would they have found still existing of the capitalist system that they had known and described? Where was free competition amid all of these monopolies? Where was economic freedom amid all of these state interventions? Where was consumer sovereignty among all of the selling campaigns practiced by the producers to shape consumers' desires? What indeed remains of the free market system when giant corporations are compelled to make long-term plans to guarantee a return on their huge investments? What indeed remains of the capitalist system? To be sure, ownership of the means of production remains essentially private, and the incentive for investment and production remains the maximization of profit. But which is more important, the legal form of ownership (whether private or public), or the degree to which it has spread in the society and the degree to which private ownership has become subjected to the demands of public interests?

What has to be admitted is that by the mid-twentieth century the capitalist system was a very different thing from what it had been one hundred years earlier. Many books have indeed been published that attempt to draw attention to these important differences, written by both Marxists and liberals. Marxists Sweezy and Baran published a book in the early 1960s entitled *Monopoly Capital*, in which they explained the changes that had taken place since Marx's *Das Kapital* was published a hundred years earlier. The Keynesian economist John Kenneth Galbraith in the late 1960s published *The New Industrial State*, also to explain the changes that had come about in the capitalist system. Both books talked about very profound changes in the capitalist system, but neither one claimed that the capitalist system had fallen, as Marx had predicted, nor suggested giving the capitalist system another name.

The reason is that neither the friends nor the enemies of capitalism would have liked either possibility. Supporters of capitalism would not like to admit that Marx's predictions of the fall of capitalism had any validity whatever, nor would they like openly to concede that the system has become much closer to monopoly than to perfect competition. Nor would they like, of course, to admit that the sovereign is no longer the consumer but the producer, nor that producers have often come to rely heavily on the state for help. Nor do the enemies of capitalism like to admit that the system has become more humane than before and may therefore deserve a better name.

It is worth noting, however, that although these changes have taken place in the capitalist system without any explosion of the type predicted by Marx, they have to a large extent been produced by the same conditions that Marx predicted would bring about the change: increased disparity in income. For it does seem impossible that the capitalist system, or any other system for that matter, can sustain more than a certain degree of income disparity without curtailing growth.

The second half of the twentieth century brought new changes to the socialist and capitalist systems alike. Perhaps the most important of these changes are related to a higher rate of globalization. The development of methods of production and the advances achieved in communications and information technology have propelled production and consumption to become much more global than at any time in the past. This has encouraged a rapprochement between the two camps of East and West, widely known as the socialist and capitalist, for while the former was badly in need of the technology of the latter, the latter badly needed the markets of the former. Thus, barriers have fallen and important governments were changed. But to what extent can one regard what happened as a triumph of capitalism over socialism, as Marx and Engels would have understood the two terms? Has free competition (one of the most important distinguishing characteristics of capitalism in Marx's conception) replaced state monopolies over the means of production or in the taking of investment and production decisions (one of the most important distinguishing characteristics of socialism in his conception), or was what happened rather that private monopolies have taken the place of state monopolies? Has the authority in deciding what to produce and how much, returned to the consumer, or have private companies usurped the role of the state in commanding the obedience of consumers? Has central planning been replaced by the dictates of the market or has corporate planning taken the place of government planning, both being quite comprehensive and central? Has the role of government intervention in the economy been taken away, or does it remain decisive but serving the interests of large corporations, especially when these interests require launching a war and greater production of weapons?

The fact is that the capitalism that conquered the Eastern bloc countries bears little resemblance to the capitalism described by the classical economists, and the socialist governments that fell in the last quarter of the twentieth century bore little resemblance to the socialism envisioned by Marx and Engels. For all of that, capitalism's enthusiasts, or, more precisely, proponents of the system prevalent today in the Western industrialized world led by the United States, find it convenient to continue using the term capitalism for the system that conquered the Eastern bloc, and like to regard the governments that fell as representing socialism, despite all of the changes that have taken place in the capitalist system since Marx and Engels and the classical economists wrote about it and despite the distance that separated the system applied by the former Soviet Union from that envisioned by Marx and Engels.

Be that as it may, the truth is that neither the system that fell nor the system that won bears much resemblance to the systems discussed a hundred and fifty years ago. What is more, it is very hard indeed to describe the changes that have happened in the two systems as constituting overall progress or its opposite. For no one can be certain that the system prevailing today in either group of countries is more or less desirable than that which prevailed fifty or a hundred years ago.

7

Human Rights

Human needs are indeed numerous, but human needs are one thing and human rights are another. A need does not become a right unless it is recognized as such by a group of people. In other words, to recognize a certain need as a right implies that it acquired legal status within a group of people (whether it is a nation, a tribe, a family, a union, or a club) that such a need should be met. It follows that rights may be narrower or wider than needs. You may be badly in need of something that no one recognizes as your right to receive. This would be a need but not a right, an example being the case of slaves in a society that only recognizes the rights of the freeborn. Alternatively, others may recognize your right to something that cannot be construed as a need at all, as when a society recognizes the right of people to drink alcohol in public and punishes anyone who tries to impede that.

It should follow from this that human societies and cultures are bound to disagree widely among themselves about what they do and do not regard as human rights. True, it is easy for all to agree on what are and are not human needs, but we cannot expect all societies across the ages, in differing geographical and economic conditions, in different stages of economic development, and of various faiths and creeds, to recognize the same individual rights. What Muslims regard as human rights cannot be the same as what Christians or Buddhists regard as such, just as an African tribe at a very early stage of technological development must define human rights differently from an American or a Swede.

For that reason, I find it most surprising that human rights are often written and spoken about as if their recognition and definition are a foregone conclusion, as if all peoples, societies, and cultures should understand the expression 'human rights' in a single way and all agree on its implications. If an American woman walks down a public street with her legs bare and someone criticizes her for it, or she is arrested for not covering up, she is sure to demand her human rights and to protest anyone's interfering in her private affairs. What is more, the vast majority of Americans would probably support her in that attitude. On the other hand, it would never occur to an Arab woman to walk in such a manner of dress down the street in an Arab village, or to feel that engaging in such behavior would be exercising her personal freedom, or that whoever prevented her from doing it was violating one of her human rights. If she did think that, most people in the society would not lend her support.

In the Arab family, it is considered the right of sons and daughters that the family provide for their needs until the son finishes his education and until the daughter marries; this is considered to be among the rights due to them, or rather, one of their human rights, by virtue of their young age. In American families, on the other hand, the father and mother may part with their children at a relatively young age, and the children may even be encouraged to earn their living before completing their education. In Asian and African families, it is considered the right of the elders to live with their children, no matter how much of a burden that presents, but neither American nor European families see this as a human right. It is true that cultures agree to a large extent on what constitutes the basic needs of children or of the elderly, but they diverge widely on what they consider their rights, depending, as we have seen, on varying social, economic, and historical circumstances.

For that reason, I am quite amazed at the conceit with which some countries in this day and age try to foist their conception of human rights on the rest of creation as if the effluvia of their own culture are the last word in human wisdom, civilization, and rationality. Indeed some countries, together with some international organizations, are today trying to define what are to be considered human rights and to assess which countries are and which are not observing them. Such an attitude would be amusing were it not so maddening.

Another thing that invites derision and exasperation is the widespread persistence today of understanding human rights as if they were limited to one's rights against the state, especially the right of people to freedom from government interference, as if the state were the sole source of enmity toward human rights. In fact, as I had an occasion to mention in an earlier chapter, the threats are many because the causes of being denied the ability to fulfill their needs are also many, and the state is only one of these causes. The source of workers' inability to meet all of their needs could be employers who exploit them and not the state. The source of the denial of women's right to dignity could be the media and not the state. The source of readers' inability to meet their needs for independent thought could be the newspapers or television. The denial of city residents' right to peace and quiet may be microphones and not the state.[17] The source of violations of a human's need for privacy is not the state but merely population pressure.

The state is not the only, nor indeed necessarily the most important, source of violations of human rights, as some writers on human rights seem to believe. Hence the attempt to depict China's restrictions on expression and demonstrations as the single most reprehensible example of violations of human rights is almost comical. It follows that reducing government interference is not by any means synonymous with greater respect for human rights. Indeed, increased government involvement could be crucial to ensuring respect for some rights and to fulfilling some basic human needs, as humanity has known for a long time, at least since the pharaonic age.

For these reasons I find the current insistence on the need to respect human rights, as a specific collection of rights that should demand the same degree of respect in all countries by all cultures and at any time, highly misleading. And it is particularly humiliating to see one culture singling itself out, and giving itself the right to act as a policeman responsible for enforcing what it calls human rights, when these are often no more than the rights recognized by this particular culture, which happens to be, at this particular point in history, the most advanced economically and with the greatest military power.

8

The Information Revolution

On August 4, 2002, something horrible happened to two English girls, Jessica and Holly, which caused the whole country to tremble, and the British people could not stop talking about it for several weeks. When they woke up in the morning, they would remember Jessica and Holly. When they met friends, they would ask, "What is the latest news about Jessica and Holly?" When they got into taxis, they would ask the driver, "Has Huntley been charged yet?" and they could be sure that the driver would know who Huntley was and what they meant by his being charged.

Despite people's preoccupation with it, it quieted down when the press was advised that any more talk about the man and woman accused of the crime could compromise the court proceedings completely and would expose the news media itself to the accusation of obstructing justice.

Jessica and Holly were two pretty little girls, and the picture that the press kept printing of them and that was plastered all over shop windows and buses spoke of their innocence and optimism, the like of which we see in the faces of the great majority of children their age. They were about ten, neighbors, and inseparable friends. They went to the same school, loved playing computer games, and they would often go together to the nearby shop to buy sweets. Half an hour before they disappeared, they were at a small family barbecue in the garden of one of them. It was on a Sunday, about 5:30 p.m., when their families saw them for the last time; they thought that the girls had gone off to buy some sweets as usual and that they would return soon. They never did.

The news first began to be published in the inside pages of newspapers telling of the disappearance of two girls of about ten. This kind of thing is not unheard of in England, and the story might have been treated like most other stories of disappearance or murder—a small story, soon forgotten. Here, however, some decision-maker at one of the papers must have seen the makings of a press sensation. Maybe their picture evoked the idea. It was as I have described it, a picture of gentleness and innocence, but they were also wearing similar shirts, both red and emblazoned with the emblem of the enormously popular soccer club, Manchester United. The story thus carried many of the elements that were bound to attract the attention of a huge readership. It brought together those particulars that guarantee people's continued interest: sex, violence, and fear of death, combined with two pretty, typically British faces, and on top of it all, the name of the beloved soccer club.

Not surprisingly, the picture was published the next day on the front page. Naturally, what one paper does the others cannot fail to follow, lest readers abandon them. Suddenly, publishing the picture of the two girls dressed in red, together with the latest developments in the search for them, became a daily obligation for every paper (as well as for television).

The following day, a picture of the parents of both girls was also published for the first time, all four of them standing side by side in front of the lens. There was no apparent sense of grief about them but merely despondency and lack of comprehension. They were obviously not ready for this situation, and the media caught them unawares, looking like normal people with nothing to distinguish their faces from the millions of other people seen every day in the streets.

For two or three days, the hope persisted that the two girls might still be found alive and the whole affair would end up an unpleasant joke, a stupid idea that perhaps came over one of the girls, which they pulled off without telling anyone about it. Then the papers started publishing pieces about a letter that one of the mothers addressed to the person who may have kidnapped them, begging him to return her daughter to her. Some people thought that it might be a good idea to solicit the help of the famous soccer player David Beckham, whom the crowds worshipped and who played for the same club the girls fancied. Thus, some paper published a letter from Beckham addressed to the two girls asking them to return to their families, in the hope that their disappearance might have been their own doing and not a kidnapping. With that, the papers were killing two birds with one stone: cashing in on the public appeal of the incident as well as on the celebrity of the soccer player.

The situation took a brand new turn however, and blew into a public spectacle in the true sense of the word when two newspapers launched a competition, one of them announcing a million-pound reward to whoever could give information leading to the discovery of the two girls, and the other quickly making a similar announcement but with a smaller reward. From that point on, the situation was transformed from a mystery crying out for a solution into something akin to rabble-rousing. From there, it became a matter of pure profit maximization, with the sole goal of increased circulation of the papers. A private tragedy was thus transformed into a soap opera followed hour by hour by millions in Britain and abroad. The media exploited the insatiable desire of people for thrills, even when that meant gawking at the disasters befalling others. The greater the legions of people following the story, the greater became the media's lust for milking the numbers for increased profits. The public spectacle inspired dismay more than pain and excitement more than grief, giving way to even more tragedies than the grief brought about by the original incident.

The whole thing brings to mind the story of the unfortunate Princess Diana, from the time she was divorced from the crown prince until she was killed in an automobile accident. For here again it was impossible to separate the events in the princess's life after her divorce until her death from what the media did to her. They transformed her personal life with all of its details into news stories followed by millions of people who had not the least connection to her. They transformed her from just a good, simple, pretty woman into an actress always on camera and lionized in the press. This surely had an effect on her behavior, ending in her death in an accident caused by the press pursuing her car, which was speeding to get away from it. Here, too, we find that what started as a personal tragedy was transformed by the mass media into another, and maybe worse kind of tragedy.

This, of course, is what George Orwell wanted to say in his famous essay, "Shooting an Elephant," which tells the story of a policeman sent to track a rogue elephant running loose in the lanes of an Asian village and to do what he could to bring it under control without killing it, unless absolutely necessary. Upon hearing the news, masses of people set out after the policeman in his pursuit of the elephant, growing in number from a few hundred to several thousand, for whenever some saw a large group of people heading off in a particular direction, they would fall in behind them to find out what was going on, all of them looking for excitement and waiting for the sight of a dead elephant. That put the policeman in a position where he had no choice but to shoot the elephant, even when this was not at all necessary to bring it under control. The decisive factor in such a tragic outcome was merely that of numbers: the number of spectators hoping to witness the killing.

In the case of Holly and Jessica, as soon as the two newspapers announced the huge cash rewards to whoever could provide information leading to the arrest of the perpetrator, police stations were hit by an avalanche of calls and electronic messages from all and sundry imagining that they possessed some useful information, with the number of contacts averaging more than a thousand a day. This put the police in a bind. It was certain that most of the calls and messages were of no use whatsoever, their only motivation being the hope for a reward or simply the chance to take part in the public hullabaloo. But it was also possible that some of the information might be useful, even if it were only one message, and the police officers would not be able to forgive themselves if they ignored it. The problem was how to distill that one message out of the thousands upon thousands of others. There was nothing for the police to do save to increase the number of people involved in the search for the victims and in vetting the messages. Thus, they recruited forces from outside their jurisdiction, indeed from outside of the police force altogether. They requested aid from the army and the use of new equipment that had never been intended for such purposes.

One day followed another with no breakthrough, no clue coming to light, nor any thread that might lead the police to the perpetrator or to the whereabouts of the girls. A taxi driver reported that he had seen a green car in which a man was trying to take control of two children. For one reason or another, the police disregarded this piece of information for more than a week, but then they were forced to investigate, as some of the papers had started blaming the police for ignoring this important bit of evidence. It then turned out that the time in which the driver witnessed the incident conflicted with the known time of the disappearance of the girls, thus this bit of information was completely dismissed. After that, a woman volunteered that she had been sitting in a restaurant some hours after the girls had disappeared and had seen another woman get up to leave, giving the patrons of the restaurant a strange look. The police set about looking for a woman with a strange look, but of course, with no result.

People started grumbling; the easiest thing was to accuse the police of dereliction and inefficiency. Some of them said that the problem was that Britain did not have a body like the FBI in the United States and that it was high time that such a body was formed. They failed to consider the number of similar unsolved crimes that take place in the United States every day. The police resorted to a different tactic. They announced a public meeting for an exchange of views among the inhabitants of the village of Soham, where the crime took place. Men and women came, some bringing their children with them, to hear what the police had to say. The policeman in charge informed them that the perpetrator of the crime must be one of them, that he was undoubtedly from the same village, and that he knew the two girls well. He said that the people of the village should begin to look around at their neighbors and even at their relatives, as most such crimes are committed by a close male relative of the victim, sometimes one of the closest. Some of those present began to ask themselves, "Have we really descended to this state? Have we finally entered the age of Big Brother, in which everyone spies on one another, even on one's own parents, and reports to the police any doubt that comes to mind about the behavior of those closest to them?"

The surprising thing is that not one newspaper, television, or radio commentator speculated about the significance of the effects of this mass hysteria on the actions of people, the police, and the media. The most one or two writers did was to touch lightly upon the subject, one writer using the term Big Brother without elaboration when referring to the meeting. That was because the writers were themselves afraid of the throng. Who would be bold enough to defy public sentiment by expressing anything other than grief and pity over the disappearance of the girls? Did the writer have no feelings? In the face of the horrible nature of the crime could one still find it within oneself to complain about the public clamor affecting police behavior and the media? Is this the time for that? What kind of paper would publish such things, even if its employees did write them?

A man went to the police saying that he had seen a field a few miles out of Soham that looked as if it had been "disturbed"; that is, there had been a recent excavation there. An uproar ensued. The media in their flurry kept repeating the words "disturbed ground," and all eyes looked toward the police as they descended on the spot to search for anything, announcing that they would be searching all night by spotlight and that the families of the two girls would be notified if they found anything. When the sun rose, the police had found nothing.

At long last we heard exciting news: the police were questioning a young man in his late twenties, by the name of Ian Huntley, who worked as a caretaker at a local high school, and his fiancée Maxine Carr, also in her late twenties, who was a teacher's aid at the school which the lost girls attended. The police were not saying what had led them to question these two specifically. The next morning, people saw pictures of Huntley and Maxine in the papers, two completely normal people no different from thousands of others seen every day. That is how the matter rested after the police announced that they had released the two after asking them some questions. Indeed, the newspapers published remarks of some of the couple's neighbors saying that they were very nice, mild-mannered people. The papers also published a picture of a greeting card that one of the lost girls had sent to Maxine, in which she expressed love for her in her capacity as a teacher's aide at her school.

The situation changed completely a few hours later, when the police announced that they had arrested Huntley on the charge of murdering the girls. A few days later, they announced the arrest of Maxine, charging her with obstruction of justice. This time when the press published their pictures, they chose pictures in which the two looked a little odd. Thus, when the public saw the pictures for the second time, they did not see the faces of two normal young people; instead, they saw two people who might not be perfectly normal and who might be criminals. The police gave no details about what Huntley had done or what Maxine had said to obstruct the investigation, nor did they say what the committed crime was exactly, how it had been carried out, or what the motives were. The police suppressed all of this information as if they had decided that the media had exceeded its bounds, and that it was time to stop it. The police seemed to think that a fair trial had been made almost impossible because of the clear bias that had been spread among the people against the accused, even before the public knew precisely what they had done, and that the defense could claim the same and get the two off.

Consider the hysteria that gripped people when they saw Maxine leaving in a police vehicle to go to the police station to hear the charges against her. They showered her with abuse, calling her the most abominable names and throwing at her whatever they could find. Were it not for the alert protection of the police, they would have killed her in an instant. When the papers published the pictures of the mob clamoring for a return of the death penalty by hanging, we witnessed people as close to enraged animals as they could become, their faces animated with passions no less criminal than we might have expected to see on the faces of Jessica and Holly's killers.

The newspapers also saw fit to publish new pictures of the girls' parents. It was easy to see the change that had come over the faces of the four of them after all these weeks and even the changes in the clothes they wore. They had been transformed in the space of not more than three weeks into something close to film stars, they and the saintly Jessica and Holly. And film stars cannot appear before the public in the same clothes that they wear in their everyday lives. Some papers published appeals from the two families to the media to respect their right to privacy and quiet, and to leave them alone to reflect upon their grief in peace. To no avail. Their appeal was like that of one who raises his voice in a public square amid a clamorous crowd of thousands of demonstrators who have lost their reason.

Some days passed, and then the papers published and the television broadcast pictures of the church where thousands of bouquets of flowers were brought from near and far by people expressing their commiseration with the families of the girls and their grief over what had happened. Of course, the small local church could not accommodate all the people coming to pay their condolences and to pray, so it was decided to open the great cathedral at Ely nearby. That vast church too was overwhelmed with people, and it too was unable to accommodate all of the mourners.

The matter did not end there. Soham became famous, and hundreds of visitors came every day to see the village that by now had acquired an awe and respect that other British cities of larger size and longer history did not enjoy. Thus, there came into being a new phenomenon that some papers labeled 'crime tourism.' This caused one of the clergy members of Soham to make an impassioned appeal to visitors to respect the memory of the two girls and the feelings of the townspeople and to cease certain activities, such as playing ball in the field next to the church and listening to loud music.

This, then, is how the mass media, in the age of what is called the communications and information revolution, transformed a truly horrible incident, but one that directly affected only a small number of people, into a mass happening of historical proportions with features of farcical comedy, all for the sake of increased profits. But this media revolution encapsulates yet another tragedy different from that which struck the girls and their families. The tragedy is that even though the incidence of kidnapping children has not increased in Britain over the last ten years—it has remained steady or even declined—the media's way of treating kidnappings, with the relentless presentation at which the broadcast and print media have proved so successful, has sparked unprecedented fear and worry in the country. It is difficult amid such hysteria for anyone to think statistically and to realize that the great majority of children are exposed to no danger and that most adult men are normal and pose no threat to children. The way in which the media treat such incidents, however, causes people to suppose that such tragedies are the rule and that anything else is the exception, and worry and fright spreads. Mothers and fathers cling tightly to their children's hands and forbid them from going out except in their company. Parents advise their children not to speak with strangers and even to doubt those closest to them. Do not the media say that such caution is necessary? What is more, how can children be protected from what the television broadcasts about such incidents? This compelled one mother to ask a newspaper correspondent, "What are we to tell our children now?"

Mothers and fathers who took their children with them to those noisy demonstrations of mourning were probably thinking that it is the right of children to know everything, as it is ours, as the media keep telling us, perhaps regarding getting such information as yet another human right. Perhaps it is, but what sort of men and women will these children grow into as a result of all this?

9

Ethics

When the news began to come out that an effort
would be made to change the religious instruction
curriculum in Egyptian schools to allow ethics to replace
religion as such, as well as to allow Muslim and Coptic students to attend the same classes together, read the same
texts, and sit for the same examinations, I did not regard
this as a good sign. An incident that happened to my father
long ago leaped to my mind and kept coming back to me
time after time, which created in me a feeling of unease
about what the ultimate outcome of all this might be.

It is not hard for all of us to agree that there is a close
relationship between the feeling of having a moral duty
and having a sense of loyalty. The existence of a feeling of
loyalty seems to be a necessary condition for the existence
of a moral duty, perhaps a necessary as well as a sufficient
condition. It is indeed hard to imagine a moral obligation
without some kind of loyalty, but it is probably also true
that to have a sense of loyalty must imply the existence of
a moral duty.

By loyalty I mean a mixture of a feeling of belonging to
a human grouping–family, tribe, sect, party, or nation–
together with a feeling of responsibility for the welfare of

that group. It can be said that the combination of these two feelings creates a sense of loyalty. Wherever that is found, what we may call a moral sense is also to be found, represented by feelings of obligation to undertake certain types of behavior and to eschew other types, not for fear of the law or the expectation of a reward, but simply due to a sense of propriety.

It is not hard, therefore, to show how the ethical sense (or a sense of propriety) might be developed, strengthened, weakened, or eliminated. For the question about how an ethical sense is developed turns into a question about how a sense of loyalty appears and develops. It should not be difficult to demonstrate how a sense of loyalty begins to appear in early childhood, as a feeling of belonging and accountability develops as a result of repeated shared experiences with others, and in being exposed to the same sources of joy and pain or the same hazards and expectations. Such feelings begin usually in the home among family members, and then among schoolmates and in early friendships. At the same time, a sense of loyalty to the nation is formed as individual citizens share in experiences of and sentiments about whatever is happening to the homeland, the hazards confronting it, and the goals it aspires to. Throughout all of this, and from the beginning of awareness of the religious rites and customs observed by their families, children also develop a sense of belonging to and accountability toward their religion and toward those who share the same faith.

We also know that a sense of ethical obligation may exist vis-à-vis people who are not members of one's family or schoolmates, coreligionists, or members of the same ethnicity, but merely out of the shared ties of humanity, hence also a sense of belonging and accountability, although admittedly such sentiments are usually weaker than those felt toward family members, friends, and members of the same nation or religion. We also know that many are capable of feeling moral obligations to animals, and that such feelings can develop with long association, especially as certain animals seem to their owners to be able to distinguish them from others, which strengthens the feelings of belonging and loyalty.

In the light of this, I think we can understand why one may have strong doubts about the veracity of those who claim they feel no moral obligation to their nuclear family, nation, or religion, but feel it instead toward humanity in general, and may view such claims as no more than deception. It is perfectly true that large numbers of people, especially in wealthy countries, donate to the victims of natural disasters or wars that afflict other people than their own, and that many volunteer for rescue work among those unlucky people without expecting reward or fearing reprisal, motivated only by common ties of humanity. We also know about animal rights movements and the concern expressed for animals threatened with extinction. No doubt, many individuals in these movements are motivated by a moral sense not too different from that which motivates others to sympathize with other human beings. Nevertheless, it is also true that these instances of the moral sense are more rare than the feeling of sympathy for one's own human group, whether it be the family, a national collective, or members of the same religion.

If all this is true, how can the moral sense be strengthened, should we wish to strengthen it, and how are some forms of moral behavior to be spread, if that is what we desire?

The answer that seems to follow from the above is to strengthen feelings of loyalty and belonging. Anything that strengthens family ties will also strengthen the sense of moral obligation among its members toward one another, and the same thing must be true of national and religious ties.

Fortunately, the strengthening of the feeling of belonging and loyalty to a relatively small circle does not necessarily involve the weakening of feelings of loyalty to larger groupings of people. The strengthening of the moral sense toward family members does not necessarily involve a weakened moral sense toward the nation, coreligionists, or humanity in general. It appears that human beings are fortunately capable of combining such a variety of feelings of loyalty without one of them necessarily obliterating the others. Indeed it often happens that the strengthening of the sense of moral obligation in any particular grouping of people leads to a stronger sense of moral obligation to other broader or narrower groupings of people. Nevertheless, we must admit that the matter largely depends on the means by which strengthening the feeling of loyalty takes place. There are, of course, ways of strengthening this sense of loyalty that involve inciting enmity and hatred of others, such as fomenting nationalist fervor by scorning and criticizing the enemy, or attracting the support of coreligionists by condemning or belittling other religions. It is difficult to speak unreservedly of this approach as strengthening the moral sense, as it leads to losing from one hand what has been gained in the other. Such fears are undoubtedly justified but we must admit the peril of taking this too far. There are those who assert that it is dangerous to strengthen loyalty to particular groupings (such as a nation or religious group) on the ground that this might weaken the sense of moral obligation to others (other nations or faiths). True, there is such a risk, but the situation depends on how loyalty is instilled. It would indeed be a great pity, or so it seems to me, if the fear of such an error led to a weakening of loyalty to one's own human group, be it a nation or members of the same faith. And it would be an even greater pity if it led to the weakening of the moral sense altogether, in whatever manifestation.

Let me now tell the story that the issue of teaching ethics rather than religion in schools brought back to me. In his autobiography, *My Life*, my father, Ahmed Amin, had something to say about the teaching of ethics at the school for *shari'a* judges at the beginning of the twentieth century, almost exactly a century ago now. That was the school from which my father graduated after studying at al-Azhar and in which he worked as a teacher until he went to teach at the Egyptian University (now Cairo University). The superintendent of the school was Atef Barakat, a man of high integrity and wide knowledge, who left a profound impression on my father, so much so, that he called him his "second, spiritual father."

Barakat was fascinated by the culture of the West, especially by the English, and he did not have, at heart, much respect for his own traditional culture, even if he did not always allow himself to express that. Thus, when he saw that ethics was being taught by a sheikh with a traditional educational background, and from an old but widely respected Arabic book called *Adab al-dunya wa-l-din* (Principles of Worldly and Religious Behavior), written in the fifth century *hijri*, the tenth century AD, by Abu al-Hasan al-Mawardi, he was not particularly happy, took charge of the situation, and started teaching ethics out of English-language books written by well-known utilitarians including John Stuart Mill. When my father was appointed as Barakat's assistant, he began to be invited to his house so that they could prepare the lessons in ethics together, exclusively from English books. My father tells of it thus in his autobiography:

> He would read in English and dictate to me in Arabic, sometimes translating himself and reading to me his translation. Then we would discuss the lesson before he delivered it. . . . He had a great influence on me in subjecting religion to reason. Until that time I had been ruled by emotion not by the mind, and I had not allowed myself to debate such issues with rational arguments.

The intellectual transformation that my father underwent as he went from reading al-Mawardi to reading Mill caught my attention. I could not help recalling my own reading of Mill as he described his intellectual transformation while reading Jeremy Bentham, the English social philosopher and founder of utilitarianism. It was impossible to avoid noticing that the reason behind this intellectual transformation was the same with my father as it was with Mill, and the profundity of its influence was also similar. In both cases the transformation consisted of a revolt against metaphysics in favor of the secular, and against the reliance on received wisdom in favor of using one's own mind. There is obviously something very seductive about such a move, even when, as in the case we are now discussing, it is applied not to the study of nature or of society but to ethical judgment, where one may indeed wonder whether such a move should be welcome.

Bentham was searching for a ruling principle for ethics resembling the ruling principle in Newtonian physics and found it (or he thought he had) in the principle of utility. Acts are to be judged as good or bad according to the degree to which they fulfill this universal good: "The greatest happiness for the largest number." Simply by stumbling upon this formula, Bentham thought he had found the hidden treasure that he had been seeking, and he was ready to sing for joy. James Mill, the father of John Stuart Mill, also sang for joy when he heard it from Bentham, and the same thing happened to John Stuart Mill once he heard it from his father. So did my father when he heard it from his mentor, Atef Barakat, who gave him Mill's book to read.

I can clearly imagine the enthusiasm of my father on his first encounter with utilitarianism, which happened when he was no more than twenty years old, and what his feelings were when he compared it to al-Mawardi's work. I also know from Mill's autobiography the enthusiasm he felt when he first encountered utilitarianism before he had turned twenty. My father wrote a book about ethics some years after his conversion and the book was used in the 1940s as a textbook in Egypt's secondary schools. Simply entitled *Ethics*, it was a sympathetic explanation of Bentham's principles, and it never mentioned al-Mawardi's name.

When I first read this story about Barakat and the teaching of ethics in my father's autobiography, I had some idea about utilitarianism as Bentham and Mill had expounded it, but I had never read anything by or about al-Mawardi. This was exactly the opposite of what had happened with my father's education. Whereas he had first studied in the tradition of al-Mawardi and then been exposed to the English tradition, I had since childhood been exposed from various quarters to Western culture, disregarding the sources of my own tradition, except in the Arabic language and religion classes.

The story created in me a strong desire to read al-Mawardi's book. Fortunately, it was easy to find a copy and I set about reading it. I found it a great book and it left a great impression on me, reflecting as it did immense learning, wisdom, and admirable perception of human nature, and written in beautiful Arabic. Here is one story which it relates to illustrate one moral principle and which I choose here at random just to give the reader the flavor of the book.

> Ibn Qutayba tells of 'Umar ibn al-Khattab,[18] may Allah be pleased with him, that he happened to pass by some boys playing, among them Abdallah ibn al-Zubayr. They all ran away from him except for Abdallah. So Omar

said to him, "What is the matter? Why do you not run from me the way your friends did?" Whereupon the boy answered, "O Leader of the Faithful, I had not committed any wrong so as to fear you, nor is the road narrow, so as to move to make room for you."[19]

The book is full of such stories expressing noble sentiments. That being the case, I wondered what it was that made Barakat dismiss it so easily? He probably saw two things in it that he did not like. First, it is a book of literature that addresses ethical questions, and he wanted ethics to be studied as a science, something he thought he found in Bentham and John Stuart Mill. Second, it is a book that sought inspiration in Islamic and Arab culture and was full of respect for and loyalty to that culture, while he wished for a textbook on ethics to transcend loyalty to any particular culture and hence to appeal to students of any community or religion, exactly as some people now wish to replace the teaching of religion in Egyptian and Arab schools with general textbooks of ethics that address all religions and cultures.

For my part, I tend toward caution on both counts. As for turning ethics from a literary subject into a scientific discipline, I have some reservations, for a start, about how to classify al-Mawardi's book. In addition to being a fine work of literature, with quotations from the best classical Arabic poetry and prose, the book is also full of pieces of social analysis and sound judgment on social issues distilled from very wide reading in history and trenchant reflections on human nature. Should all this be dismissed so easily on the ground of being 'unscientific'?

But regardless of the proper classification of al-Mawardi's book, can ethics truly be treated as a science without losing its most important and most attractive features? What exactly have we gleaned from Bentham's principle of "the greatest happiness for the largest number"? That measure is ultimately based on a comparison between total pleasure resulting from any action and total pain, making allowance for the strength and the durability of the pleasure and the pain. No distinction is made, however, between one kind of pleasure and another or one kind of pain and another with respect to any other goal than maximum pleasure or satisfaction. There is, no doubt, an interesting intellectual exercise to be had, but the application of the principle provides no way of deciding between two unequal actions from any other angle than their utility. If we define utility as whatever we find agreeable, the principle becomes simply a reiteration of the self-evident. Aside from that, the principle has been, and may continue to be, employed to justify any unethical action in the name of increasing utility.

If this is the case, it would seem to be a huge mistake to try to free ethics from any cultural or religious context. If what I said at the beginning of the chapter is true, that ethics must necessarily be intertwined with a sense of loyalty to a particular religion, culture, or social group, then to free ethics from those bonds would most probably weaken the moral sense rather than strengthen it. The old saying that a skeleton key opens all doors applies here: a person who belongs to all of humanity without feeling any sense of belonging to any particular culture, religion, or community is probably one with no loyalty or sense of belonging of any sort.

The cure for bigotry is not to weaken ties of loyalty but to encourage the use of the intellect and the application of wisdom in assuming and expressing loyalty to keep it from being transformed into a vehicle for hate. To strengthen the moral sense is to implant in people a sense of loyalty to their own religions and cultures without prejudice against adherents of other religions or members of other cultures. This is not impossible or even difficult to achieve; we in Egypt knew such a climate of loyalty to faith, culture, and country tempered by reason and tolerance just before the current wave of intolerant xenophobia started to hit us some thirty years ago.

The generation of Bentham at the end of the eighteenth century and the beginning of the nineteenth century, as well as the succeeding generation of John Stuart Mill, felt great confidence in the power of the values of the Enlightenment and of education, and they were supremely confident in the power of reason and science for promoting morality. What actually happened seems to be closer to the exact opposite. The spread of the values of the Enlightenment and of education and the growth of the prestige of anything regarded as 'science,' as well as the widespread application of Bentham's utilitarianism, do not seem to have been associated with a noticeable rise in moral standards. One explanation may be the progressive weakening of the feelings of loyalty to family, nation, and religion.

10

Terrorism

-1-

What a great invention! It was not a new media device like the radio or television, nor was it a new form of rapid transit like the train or airplane, nor indeed was it some new brand of weapon. No, it was merely an idea or, to be more precise, simply a word. But it was a word that could mobilize armies, promote products, reduce unemployment, unite opposed groups within a community, win elections, and justify endless military campaigns.

The inventor cannot have been only one person, for such an invention requires the cooperation of many talented people from numerous and varied specializations. It requires experts in the fields of political science, sociology, economics, linguistics, and psychology—but especially in the workings of the human mind, which is a mysterious world full of contradictions.

The idea must have come about with the discovery of the need for inspiring fear in people. This by itself was an ingenious discovery, even if it was not easy in the first instance to discern its great benefits. Fear unites people, discourages dissent, and makes them easy to lead. It weakens people's ability to detect platitudes and to distinguish between ordinary talk and sloganeering; it renders them more ready to accept orders and to relinquish many of their freedoms.

There is hardly a more powerful or effective way to effect these things than to instill the fear of death. When we or our children are exposed to danger, we will do anything that is asked of us, including closing our eyes to things we would never have dreamed of ignoring. For example, watch people on a train if someone happens to cry out that there is a bomb under one of the seats. It may never occur to anyone to stop to consider whether the statement itself is true or false and whether the person saying it is trust-worthy, or to ask what benefit might accrue to anyone by placing a bomb on the train in the first place. The impor-tant thing is to flee to safety. In those circumstances, any passenger might be suddenly transformed into a leader who gives orders to the other frightened passengers.

To be sure, political leaders' awareness of the benefits to be reaped from keeping their charges in fear goes back a long way. Dictators as well as democratic rulers have been exploiting fear for nefarious ends since time immemorial. This manipulation increased in the twentieth-century Soviet Union, especially in the Stalin era, in Germany and Italy at the hands of Hitler and Mussolini, with Churchill in Britain, and with Roosevelt in the United States. Stalin spooked his people with the bogey of capitalism, Roosevelt with communism, and Hitler and Mussolini with both, while Churchill frightened his people with Hitler and Mussolini. This mutual intimidation between capitalism and communism persisted in what was called the Cold War for almost a half-century after the end of the Second World

War. With the fall of one communist state after another from the end of the 1980s onward, however, a new source of fear was badly needed. Indeed, the search for it must have begun even before the fall of communism. The work toward developing this new source of fear must have begun right from the start of the period of détente between the two camps at the end of the 1960s, and its cultivation proceeded little by little throughout the 1970s and 1980s. Sure enough, the twenty-first century had scarcely begun when it emerged as the main source of fear for everyone and as the axis around which foreign and domestic policies revolved in many countries. This new source of fear is called terrorism.

Notice how successful was the choice of the name. Contrary to the labels capitalism or communism, Nazism or fascism, terrorism does not point to the source of the danger nor does it describe its nature or origin. It only points to its result, which is just 'terror.' This becomes clear by comparing the two statements, 'communism is scary' and 'terrorism is scary.' The first expression contains a subject and a predicate that defines the subject. The second, on the other hand, says nothing at all; the predicate 'scary' adds no new information to the subject 'terrorism.' Both words have the same meaning. It is like saying, 'a scary thing is scary.' Similarly, to say of a person that he is a 'terrorist' does not tell us a thing about the reason for fearing him; nothing about his faith, his way of thinking, his personal characteristics, or his deeds. It only indicates the effect of those deeds: inspiring fear. This is very much like saying, not that there is a bomb under the train seat, or a firearm, or a dagger, but merely that 'there is something deadly under the seat.'

I say the choice of the name terrorism was successful for that very reason: its generality and lack of meaning and the possibility of employing it in widely different circumstances to describe situations that have nothing in common except the intent to induce fear. The difference between this new invention and the old sources of fear is not unlike the difference between the mobile telephone and the household or office telephone fixed in place. Terrorism, like the mobile telephone, can be used to reach any person in any place and its use can be changed to meet new needs. The terrorist could be in Afghanistan, Iraq, or Lebanon, depending upon need, and he could be Arab, Russian, or Spanish, according to the country that needs scaring. He could use a bomb to blow up a plane or use a knife (or even a pair of scissors) to threaten the passengers, or he might put lethal powder in a letter. The terrorist might be a single person acting alone, a political or religious group, or a state that works by agreement with individual terrorists and groups. In the latter case, the state is labeled a 'rogue state,' a label which scarcely differs from the label 'terrorist.' It means only that, for whatever reason, the state is not approved of.

The terrorist could be destitute or fabulously wealthy; he could be a natural-born criminal, a God-fearing believer, or a bigoted nationalist. What is important is not his motivations for committing certain acts but the effect such acts have on other people. The poor and destitute can be just as frightening as the very rich, and the pious can be transformed into a criminal or vice versa. Consider Osama bin Laden, for example. He began life as a carefree youth, chasing women in the pleasure spots of Beirut, and has ended up in some cave in the mountains of Afghanistan or Pakistan. He started out working in the interests of America against the Russians and then turned to working in the interests of the Palestinians against the Americans. He and his family are rich to the extent that they had developed relations with the Bush family of American presidential fame, but he is now content to break bread in some unknown hideout. The same thing could be said of Saddam Hussein, who began as a close friend of the Americans, who treated him with respect, said all sorts of nice things about him, and flooded him with economic aid and weapons. Then he was suddenly transformed into their archenemy, whom they called a monster and whom they ended up bombing.

These contradictions defy belief in the way they clash in the mind of anyone who has a modicum of reason. The fact is, however, that we tend to underestimate our capacity to entertain contradictory ideas at the same time. We think that it is only children or the feeble-minded who can contain contradictions in their small minds—such things as giant creatures flying or living in tiny bottles from which they emerge now and then, or a wicked witch that can change pretty girls into swans, or a good witch that can change a pumpkin into a coach and four horses, and so on. I do not mean just that adults and intelligent people often enjoy listening to such stories and can be lost in them, I mean that all of us continue to allow contradictions to exist in our minds and to believe things that cannot possibly be reconciled.

Consider, for example, that we have been willing to believe that the prime minister of Britain decided to send

British troops to Iraq alongside the Americans in order to 'save the Iraqis from dictatorship,' when all of political history indicates that one country's interfering in the affairs of another or declaring war upon another is never done for humanitarian reasons. Likewise, Americans and others have at one time accepted the heretofore incredible statement that Colonel Muammar Qaddafi, president of Libya, represents a threat to the most powerful nation on earth, even when it was apparent that it was the easiest thing in the world to bring him to heel or to compel him, as actually happened a little later, to sing the praises of America to the whole world. They also believed that Saddam Hussein represented a lethal threat to the world with his weapons of mass destruction, until it was admitted that it was only a small intelligence error that lent credence to this fearsome notion.

The human mind must indeed work in ways very different from what we usually assume. It turns out that, once the necessary acts and precautions are taken, it is very easy to convince people of a big lie such as that terrorism threatens the peace and security of the most powerful nations and, indeed, the peace and security of people in every place on earth.

What are these necessary acts and precautions? To start with, we should not belittle the usefulness of the unceasing repetition that something called terrorism actually exists. It seems that the human mind has a strange inclination to believe in almost anything as long as a word exists for it. If you say, for instance, that "terrorism is a horrible thing," you would not only be establishing the horror of terrorism, you would also be asserting that terrorism actually exists and denying that it is simply a ploy with which to mislead people. If you say that "most terrorists are Muslims," you would not only be saying something bad about Muslims, you would also be contending that terrorism exists. If such expressions are repeated often enough, it becomes difficult to deny the existence of terrorism, and the burden of proof is moved from those who say it exists to those who claim that it is simply an artifice.

What, then, if the repetition occurs in almost all the print and broadcast media? These media seem to have acquired greater credibility than they deserve partly as a result of the nature of their means of delivery, for modern technology seems to possess some magical attraction probably derived from our ignorance of how it works. This adds much more credibility to news reports than they would otherwise possess. This indeed has been the case since the invention of the printing press, when printed books took the place of handwritten books, and to this day they seem to inspire greater confidence simply because they have been printed on a press. Even more credible are things broadcast on the radio and television. It is as if by virtue of their being the products of more sophisticated technology they have become neutral, not subject to human caprice or bias, and are therefore objective.

Greater credibility is also bestowed on books, newspapers, and the broadcast media simply by the sheer number of their readers or audience. Is it really possible that all these masses of people who do believe the news are deceived and that I am the only one who is not? People are also more ready to believe lies that are associated with things they desire wholeheartedly or things they fear greatly. We are quite ready to believe flattering remarks aimed at us by others, even when their statements are entirely removed from reality. The same may be said of our great willingness to believe anything that confirms our fear of anything that threatens our lives or those of our children. There is also the personality of those propagating the lie. It is easy to disregard the pronouncements of a crazy person, a con man, or a swindler, but what about the pronouncements of a president or a prime minister, a popular politician or a religious personality, a brilliant journalist or a talented writer, or if the utterance came from all of them at once? First some ordinary journalist reports it, then some respected journalist picks up on it, then some president and prime minister vouch for its truth, then a well-known religious personality repeats it, and finally some acclaimed writer agrees. If the assertions of its truth are repeated day after day, month after month, who can then cast doubt on the truth of such allegations?

Needless to say, it is also easier to fool people with a big lie than with a small one. If the big lie involves the occurrence of some harm to the person saying it, the readiness to accept it becomes even greater, as the possibility of a person harming himself intentionally is obviously small. This must be the reason that in the days of Muhammad 'Ali and Khedive Ismail[20] in the nineteenth century, when the losses in their wars were high, some Egyptian peasants reverted to inflicting crippling handicaps on their sons, such as cutting off a finger or a toe, in the hope they would be excused from military service. The history of colonialism is full of such horrors, like a country sacrificing great leaders and large numbers of its soldiers to secure continued rule in a colonized country. There are also many examples of large countries sacrificing innocent citizens so as to cast the blame on their enemies in order to justify declaring war or imposing harsh measures on their own citizenry. The lie in such cases is enormously large, but for that very reason most people are ready to believe it.

Regardless of the considerations that motivate belief in the unbelievable, there are definite benefits in legitimizing what leaders say, endorsing it, and in not swimming against the tide. This probably explains a great deal of what journalists and commentators write about terrorism and terrorists. There is no better way today to guarantee publication or to gain constant speaking engagements and television appearances than to include in one's writing something about the horrid threat of terrorism or about its psychological and social causes and its historical roots.

But just as there is plenty of benefit in parroting what everybody else is saying, there could be real harm in contradicting it, especially as there are ways of intimidating the dissenters that have proved quite effective. Foremost among these is to accuse the dissenter of subscribing to conspiracy theories. It is important to note the similarity between the uses of the concept of terrorism and of the concept of conspiracy theory. Each is unclear and undefined. Each is used to describe widely different situations in order to achieve a single purpose: to inspire fear. In the first case (terrorism), the fear is of destruction and death; in the second (conspiracy theory), it is the fear of ridicule and scorn. Thus, the expression of any doubt about official interpretations of events renders one a conspiracy theorist, even though a reading of history, especially modern history, and particularly very recent history, yields many examples of official explanations conflicting with the simplest rules of logic and of politicians saying one thing today and its opposite tomorrow.

This charge of adhering to a conspiracy theory may silence the boldest critic and can make the most powerful argument look silly. Far more than a simple charge of error in judgment, it includes within it an accusation of succumbing to hallucinations, fantasies, and illusions. The fear of being accused of belief in conspiracy theories has reached such an extent that it has prevented some of the best and boldest writers and commentators from revealing the doubts in their minds.

–2–

At the beginning of August 2004, the British government announced its decision to take tough measures to reduce the danger of terrorist operations being carried out in Britain, about which it said it had recently acquired new information. On the same day, the American government announced similar measures and encouraged the American people to remain extra vigilant about terrorism. At the same time, it encouraged people to go about their ordinary lives and to go to work as usual, as if nothing were amiss (regardless of the difficulty in reconciling the two requests). Combining the aim of spreading fear with that of not disrupting everyday life, the Americans were told by one official statement after another that 'We Americans will not let a few terrorists frighten us; thanks to our alertness and the watchfulness of our government, we are ready to defeat them and to wipe them out.'

I have learned not to attach too much importance to such statements because of my strong conviction that terrorism itself is basically an invention, and on that conviction, I have become accustomed not to bother reading the details of such alerts and scary declarations. Nevertheless, one day my eye fell on the front page of a widely circulated British daily newspaper, although not one of my favorites. The only story filling the entire front page was about this new and sudden British campaign against terrorism. The story began like this: "Thirteen men were arrested in a series of raids last night as armed police conducted one of the biggest operations against international terrorism in Britian. . . . The men, aged in their 20s and 30s, . . ."

I thought: There is nothing in this statement which is not to be expected. There are bound to be arrests, and the ages of the men are completely reasonable. It would not be expected that anyone under twenty would engage in terrorist acts, nor someone over forty.

The story went on: "The men, aged in their 20s and 30s, were held under the Terrorism Act 2000 on suspicion of the 'commision,' preparation or instigation of acts of terrorism."

I thought: Does this leave anything or anybody out, such as, for instance, someone like me who might be suspected of thinking about the meaning of terrorism and whether it is real or an artifice?

Then the story listed the names of some cities in which the arrests were made, among them well-known cities such as London, and lesser-known ones such as Luton, mentioning that the arrests "were part of a planned, continuing operation." That too was to be expected of such an operation, that is, that it would be "continuing," and "planned" ahead of time. The paper did not bother to mention how long the operation would be going on or when the planning for it began.

The paper went on: "It is understood that the men had been under observation for some time and the action by anti-terrorist police backed by local forces was based on information provided by the security services."

I thought: This too is logical, indeed self-evident, since it must be the function of the anti-terrorism police to arrest terrorists, the information about them must come from agencies having something to do with security, and the arrests would naturally come after a period of surveillance no matter how short. It is not a game, after all.

Up until that point, I did not feel that I had gained anything new that I might not have been able to guess before I read the piece. After that, however, the paper added some new information: "In Blackburn, there were two arrests in the Preston Old Road district. The men, of Asian origin, were held at gunpoint while travelling in a gold-coloured Mercedes at a busy junction." It is very farfetched to think that the arrest would be effected without guns being drawn. The only completely new information was the type of car and its color, gold, not red or black, as might indeed befit terrorists.

More important than anything else mentioned by the newspaper, of course, was what it said of the two suspects, that they were "of Asian origin," and that "All the suspects are of Asian origin . . ." The paper did not say who said that about the two men or who thought that about all of the suspects. It also did not mention either whether "Asian origin" might include countries such as China, Japan, and Korea or whether it was meant to apply only to Muslim countries in Asia.

Then the paper said, "The men were taken to a central London police station for questioning." adding by way of clarification that, "Today's operation is part of continuing and extensive inquiries by police and the security services into alleged international terrorism." In this manner, the paper went from one meaningless sentence to another. Perhaps because it could sense this, the paper added that Pakistani security had recently arrested a computer specialist who was believed to be connected to the al-Qaeda terrorist organization, and that in the interrogation of the man it came out that there were plans for terrorist operations in America and Britain. The newspaper, however, was obviously not bothered by one important fact that was mentioned in the same page and should have greatly weakened the story, if it did not wipe out its credibility altogether. This was the fact that this information had come from American intelligence sources, and that the American government had denied angrily what some people were saying, namely that the information contained in this piece of news was more than three years old.

The story inspired in me a powerful urge to laugh out loud, and in trying to remember anything in my experience that resembled what this newspaper was trying to pull off, I recalled my own students when they write nonsensical statements in answering some examination questions, trying to make me believe that they know something about a question when they really know nothing about it.

Throughout my long years of teaching at university, I have come across a type of student, fortunately a rare type but always an annoying one, who combines ignorance and insouciance about learning on the one hand and cunning and trickery on the other. Such students skip most lectures to spend their time playing around, but when the time comes for the exam, they sit writing and writing, one page after another in a clear, bold hand, even using multi-colored pens to underline some sentences, and all without saying anything meaningful at all. The sentences may have no meaning; they may be full of commonplaces that need no explanation or may express common knowledge possessed by the uneducated man in the street. Sentence follows sentence, repeating the same stuff, and the answer ends with a flourish punctuated with exclamation marks and underlined in red, as if the student who wrote it is very much in awe of what he has written.

Suppose the question asks the student to compare socialism and capitalism, and the student knows nothing about either. He may write something like this: "Capitalism is based upon capital, and capital is more important than anything else. The system is found in many countries of the world. In those countries, there are many rich capitalists. Socialism is the exact opposite of capitalism; it is based upon the idea of being social," and so on. Needless to say, such a student receives a zero, only because there is no lower mark to give.

I thought of such possible answers to exam questions when I read what that well-known newspaper had published on anti-terrorism measures. To be fair, I should mention that the paper did end its report with two important paragraphs that were not funny at all. On the contrary, they were distressing and inspired reflection on the truth of what is called terrorism and the fight against it:

> In May it was disclosed that 562 people had been
> arrested since September 11, 2001, under the Terrorism
> Act 2000. However, the Home Office said that fewer
> than one in five of those arrested had been charged
> under the legislation. Of the 97 charged, 14 have so far
> been convicted. Most of the charges have been for
> offences such as credit card fraud, which police suggest
> is a source of terrorist funding, and immigration irregu-
> larities. . . . Last December, 14 people were arrested in
> similar raids and most were released.[21]

In other words, a very small number of those who were at first considered terrorists had committed any crime at all. The crimes mentioned had either to do with illegal immigration to Britain (probably due to extreme poverty and not to an intent to commit terrorism) or with the use of fake or stolen credit cards. It is obvious that terrorists may very well use fake and stolen credit cards, but it is just as clear that not everyone who uses them is necessarily a terrorist.

11

Progress Backward?

In the 1930s, a mood of pessimism about the future of Europe and the world prevailed among European intellectuals. There were signs of the imminent outbreak of another war, while the horrible memories of the First World War and its millions of victims were still alive in people's minds. Reports of the abuses of human rights at the hands of the Fascists in Italy and the Nazis in Germany were increasing day by day, to which were added the dreadful news of Stalinist rule in Russia, the civil war in Spain, and the persistent economic crisis and rising unemployment throughout the Western world.

Under such conditions, it was natural that grave doubts should arise in the minds of European intellectuals about the ability of the capitalist system to bring peace and prosperity and that the great trust, prevalent in the nineteenth century, in the superiority of capitalism over any other system would be abandoned. Indeed, doubts were sure to grip them about the belief in progress itself, which had been growing in strength in Europe since the middle of the eighteenth century, when astonishing advances were made in various sciences and the industrial revolution spread from one European country to another.

One of the first to express strong doubt about the belief in progress was the English writer Aldous Huxley, even before the skies of Europe were darkened by the clouds of war, before Fascism and Nazism took root, and before the horrors of Stalinism grew to alarming proportions. Huxley gave his book, which was published in 1932, the ironic title *Brave New World*. It enjoyed wide circulation as soon as it appeared and went into new editions year after year. Then, in 1948, another English writer, George Orwell, published a novel with the unusual name *1984*. Orwell's novel expressed similar pessimism to that of Huxley, and it too achieved widespread fame and was reprinted year after year. Ever since then, the two books have been closely associated in people's minds, such that one can scarcely think of Orwell's book without calling Huxley's to mind and vice versa. Even though more than half a century has passed since the first publication of Orwell's book and more than seventy years since Huxley's, both books are still very much alive in people's minds and the question is still asked: Is today's world closer to Huxley's vision of the future or to that of Orwell? Were their frightening visions really justified?

Then the events of September 11 occurred, and interest in the two books increased again. In 2003, the centennial of Orwell's birth, the prevalent mood of worry remaining from the attacks and the resulting worrisome developments in American policy toward the rest of the world intensified interest in observation of the date. Suddenly, newspaper articles were resounding with expressions that Orwell had first coined in his novel, describing how the world might look in the future. New books came out praising Orwell's perspicacity and confirming his predictions. But some wrote that the world Huxley depicted twenty years before Orwell was closer to the world of today and that his predictions proved to be nearer the mark.

The whole issue, then, must be worthy of some contemplation. Neither Huxley nor Orwell could be treated lightly, and what happened on September 11 is not easy to forget. Just because Orwell chose the year *1984* as a title for his novel does not necessarily mean that he attached importance to that particular year or that he would have very much objected to the title being say, 2001 or 2006 instead of 1984. It is also true that Huxley's novel revolves around events that happen six centuries after Henry Ford (as the novel puts it), so we still have about five centuries left before this Brave New World of his is set to appear. Nevertheless, we should also not attach much importance to the remoteness of the date that Huxley chose for his novel. Huxley himself wrote in the introduction to the 1946 edition of the book that he had not imagined that the world might change so quickly in the fourteen years since the appearance of the first edition and that he found the world in 1946 much closer to his vision than he thought it might be after several centuries.

Let's then reconsider both books and their relationship to what has happened in the world in the wake of September 11, in the hope that this might throw new light on what is happening in the world today. For the fact is that neither Huxley nor Orwell wrote their novels simply as an exercise in imagination or for sheer entertainment. Both were enormously serious writers who possessed a high degree of moral commitment and interest in the issues of concern to their society and to humankind in general. Each of them was essentially an essayist, much more interested in writing essays than novels, and they were both well aware of this; indeed, they did not think too highly of their novels as works of literature. Huxley remarked with charming modesty that he is neither Goethe nor Dostoyevsky and that he knew well that he was not born a novelist. For his part, Orwell said when he completed *1984* that the novel was "a good idea ruined" by bad health.[22] What drove them to write novels at all was simply the thought, right or wrong, that the important message they wanted to communicate to people could more easily reach its target through novels than through essays. Each wrote his novel simply as a warning, motivated by feelings of fear and pessimism about the future if nothing were done.

What was it exactly about that future they so much feared? And is there any resemblance between what frightened them to such a degree and what has actually happened in the world since September 11? I will try to answer these questions, beginning with Aldous Huxley.

Although Huxley wrote his novel in 1931, before the peril of Nazism and Fascism appeared clearly in Germany and Italy and before Stalin had gone to such shocking extremes in Russia, Huxley had actually witnessed the beginnings of the world economic crisis, and he had lived through the tragedy of the First World War, in which he lost many friends and colleagues and in which he was prevented from participating only because of his poor eyesight. Perhaps more important, Huxley had arrived at the conviction, through his piercing insight, wide reading in many branches of knowledge, and amazing ability to draw connections between them, that progress in science and technology accompanied by an unprecedented increase in population would inevitably lead, not to an enhancement of democracy and an increase in the amount of liberty people enjoyed, but to exactly the opposite: a decline in democracy and a contraction of liberty.

In Huxley's view, scientific and technological progress leads to an ever-increasing concentration of power in the hands of a few, resulting either from a natural aptitude toward autocracy on their part, an inordinate zeal for enforcing their will upon others, or as a result of the social, political, or economic privileges they have come by. The important thing is that scientific and technological progress by nature permits the concentration of power in the hands of a few, who then force their will on others. The instruments they use are not limited to those well known in history, such as the use of weapons, prisons, or various devices of torture, but include new forms of psychological coercion. This comes with new forms of mass media and communication that influence the way people think, shape their motivations, and spread the kind of ideas, opinions, and information that those in control wish to prevail. Both types of coercion are to be found in the novels of Huxley and Orwell, but while Orwell concentrated mostly on physical coercion and torture, Huxley was more interested in psychological coercion and brainwashing.

Nowadays, based on all that has been written on the subject since the 1950s, we tend to take the influence of the mass media on people's minds for granted. Huxley was enormously forward thinking to grasp this truth so clearly and to write about it so early. In his opinion, brainwashing from an early age, or what he called "infant conditioning," was the inevitable result of scientific progress, especially in the fields of biology and psychology. Control over people's minds would not begin when they first begin reading newspapers, listening to the radio, or watching television; it was to begin at birth or even before birth. That is because the scientific progress achieved so far and the even greater achievements of the future would permit manipulation of human genes to the extent that those holding power could control human bodies and minds and shape them in any way that fit their plans.

Huxley, therefore, had good reason to be pessimistic about the future of democracy and liberty and to fear the gradual grinding down of the individual under the juggernaut of a machine-like, conformist society, where a frightening uniformity of thought and behavior prevails, individuality is suppressed, and where it becomes difficult to distinguish between one person and another.

With such advances in science and technology, no goal or principle can hold as high a place as does that of efficiency. In the end, efficiency is measured by the amount of happiness or, more properly, as stated by Jeremy Bentham more than two centuries ago, by the greatest happiness for the largest number. The greatest crime a person can commit is not to be happy. In the rare and abnormal event that someone feels unhappy, discontented, bored, or has a desire for the unattainable, the cure is quick and sure in *Brave New World*: a few grams of "soma," which, when taken, induce a pleasant stupor that lasts a few hours or days, during which all such sentiments of discontentment are erased. After that, the person who took the drug would return to normal life.

Naturally, in such a society, new attitudes would prevail toward sexuality, love, and marriage, as well as toward literature, art, and religion. Sex is practiced without any restrictions. The only abhorrent thing about sex in this society is to confine one's sexual relations to only one partner or to concentrate sexual affections on only one person. The female protagonist in the novel adopts this unconventional attitude, as it repels her to go from one sexual relation to another. Likewise, another protagonist wishes with all his heart for one particular woman and no other. Their problem is that they fall into something like love, the very emotion not understood or accepted in this technologically advanced society.

It follows from this that marriage is actually unknown, nor is there a place for the family. Indeed, the words 'father' and 'mother' have been forgotten ever since child production in test tubes began long before, whereby humans were formed according to certain known and predetermined specifications. The use of either of the terms, 'father' or 'mother,' in that society provokes feelings of embarrassment, and those who hear them blush in the same way some sexual terms may cause embarrassment in a traditional society.

In such a society, we can imagine what forms of literature and art would prevail and what would become of people's attitude toward religion. When a 'backward and primitive' person (called "the Savage" by Huxley), someone who earlier in life had read and loved the plays of Shakespeare, visits this society, his behavior and inclinations, and his quoting of scenes from Shakespeare, can only lead to surprise and scorn. There is no room in this society for the kinds of sentiment expressed by Shakespeare for there is nothing of real importance other than the attainment of happiness and pleasure and the avoidance of anything that may spoil one's mood.

Obtaining pleasure could come from listening to loud dance music or from watching diverting films in venues much like the cinemas of today, except that Huxley depicts them as always stimulating strong sensations and excitement and calls them "feelies." In that society, there is no room for religion; people do not use the name 'God,' but invoke instead the name of the captain of industry, Henry Ford. Huxley makes good use of the similarity between the automaker's name and one of the common expressions used today in reference to God: the people in his new world say "Oh Ford" instead of "Oh Lord" when expressing their surprise or fear. Moreover, they reckon events according to the number of years that have passed since the appearance of Ford, saying such and such an event occurred in the tenth or twentieth year after Ford, in the way people nowadays say something or another happened so many years after the birth of Christ.

Taken as a whole, the novel expresses Huxley's discontent with this advanced technological society. Indeed, his complete scorn for the whole idea of progress is apparent at many points in the book. In another book published in 1957, Huxley describes technological progress as merely leading the society backward with greater efficiency!

What was it exactly that made Huxley so discontented with this technologically advanced society? I think the answer is something like this: Huxley saw that every person was basically different from every other person. Just as it is impossible for one to have exactly the same face or body as another, so the moral and psychological makeup of every person is different from that of any other. If that is so, treating a group of people as if they were a homogenous unit, as if dealing with them were the same as dealing with a lifeless physical body, violates their humanity. Efficiency, in Huxley's view, is a wholly mechanistic concept: greater efficiency may increase the amount of goods and add to wealth, but it wounds humans mortally and causes them to lose something that cannot be replaced. Utilitarianism, then, is an evil philosophy in Huxley's view, at least when stripped of any other goal or ethical principle. To regard two things as achieving the same degree of contentment or happiness equally, regardless of any ethical consideration, is repugnant to Huxley, as it destroys some basic human qualities.

In 1946, just after the end of the Second World War, when Huxley sat down to write the introduction to the second edition of his book, it was clear to him (and to others like him) that the world was moving toward this frightening state of affairs much faster than he had thought. Mechanization had spread much faster than he had expected and dominated the production of goods and services; the media and the dissemination of knowledge had developed to a degree that went beyond all expectations, in addition to the destruction of lives and fortunes brought about by the Second World War. Thus the image of the future that showed itself to intellectuals after the war, especially to European intellectuals, looked more depressing than had appeared to Huxley when he first wrote his novel. It is no wonder that people read the book with greater zeal after the war than before it. Even now, more than seventy years after the first edition, it remains the only one among Huxley's novels that enjoys wide circulation.

The success achieved by *Brave New World* led Huxley to write a sequel to it in 1957 entitled *Brave New World Revisited*, in which he fleshed out his predictions of 1932 with greater detail, and more scientific and logical analysis, but with no less pessimism. In it he discusses the rapid increase of the world's population in relation to resources, the influence of technological advancement on increased regimentation and suppression, and the effect of the mass media and communication on people's thinking and on social control. When he died in 1963, Huxley's name was inextricably linked to *Brave New World*, and both his and Orwell's names continued to be evoked whenever something happened that caused people to fear the future.

———

Something like this happened on September 11, when two airplanes hit the twin towers of the World Trade Center in New York, among the tallest and most famous buildings in the world, within a short time reducing them to smoke and dust. It was certainly incredible technology, unlike anything known in Huxley's day, that made such an event possible, and the extent of human and material loss that followed was also incredible. It was scientific and technological progress that allowed destruction of such magnitude, but one should also reflect on the role of the news media and of the advance in the means of communication in governing people's emotions and in moving them in the direction defined by those with power. Identical news and commentary poured into listeners' ears and the same images appeared before their eyes, bringing the same message and fostering the same idea which those sitting at the pinnacle of rule wished to plant into people's minds. The success with which they were able to accomplish this was indeed astounding.

American youth appeared on television screens giving voice with the greatest innocence to their complete trust in what the American president had to say, while the news media, as Huxley had said in his 1946 preface to *Brave New World*, continued to avoid the discussion of any sensitive subjects that might expose the official story. As Huxley put it, "Great is the Truth, but still greater from the practical point of view, is silence about truth."[23] The trick is to keep the people of the world drowning in entertainment, now with material possessions, now with sex, now with sporting events, now with crime dramas, and so on. The feeling of fear created by the media is not only the fear of death from some act of terrorism that could happen at any moment, but also the fear of being deprived of such a great lifestyle. According to the official view, the major goal of the terrorists is to destroy the 'American way of life,' which they so greatly envy. According to this view, this was what motivated the terrorists to blow up the twin towers and the Pentagon, even though the terrorists sacrificed themselves in the process. But never mind, the government and its security agents are on the alert, and there is no reason to lose heart. In fact, there is nothing wrong with feeling secure and fearful at the same time. If the fear gets to be too much, there are drugs and drinks the effect of which is comparable to that of the 'soma' of Huxley's novel.

Despite all this, those in power cannot feel completely certain that some people, especially among the intellectuals, will not rebel, and that doubts will not spin around in their minds that what they are hearing may not exactly square with the truth. Another way of dealing with such doubters must be found besides entertainment and drugs. The solution Huxley devised in his novel is exile: moving doubters away from the ranks of the submissive, and segregating them on a remote island, where they can speak only to each other and to no one else. The risk they pose is thereby removed. This may seem too humane a way to treat recalcitrants, but we must remember that Huxley's novel was written before the world had experienced Nazism, Fascism, and Stalinism. The writer who was more suited to describing other, more violent means of suppressing opposition was George Orwell, about twenty years later.

–2–

I have read *1984* more than once, and what has always led me to reread it is the feeling that we are constantly being lied to.

I read the novel for the first time after the Israeli attack on Egypt, Syria, and Jordan in 1967. I had heard about the main idea of the book before I read it, and I was hoping to find something to help me to a true interpretation of events. I read it again after Saddam Hussein's invasion of Kuwait in 1990, when I could not believe Saddam Hussein's justifications for the invasion, as reported by the Western and Iraqi media alike. Then I read the novel again after the events of September 11, when I also could not believe what was said about the terrorist group that mounted the attack, that they it was all made up of Arabs and Muslims, who planned and executed their operation for the greater glory of Islam or as an act of revenge against America and Israel or in envy of 'the American way of life.' They certainly failed to attain any of these goals.

Of course, I never expected the novel to provide complete answers to my questions. How could it when it was written more than half a century before? But it was indeed helpful in furthering my understanding of what was going on. It further confirmed my belief in Orwell's view that the best book is that which tells you what you already know. So, what was it that

I found in this novel to throw light on the events of September 11 that differed from the official pronouncements and widespread interpretation of events?

In the first place, the novel supported my belief in the truth of what is usually referred to as 'conspiracy theories,' not in the meaning ascribed to them by their opponents—that is, diabolical meetings in dark rooms with the purpose of hatching criminal plots for advancing personal gain—but in a much simpler meaning: that behind many political acts said to be of the noblest intent are hidden selfish aims which are directly opposed to the interests of those for whom the policies are announced. This is precisely what Orwell states in his novel. The real aim of continuous war, as he says, has nothing to do with the desire for peace or for the toppling of a corrupt regime to establish a more decent one in its place. The real aim is to procure a scarce raw material or a cheap labor force; even more important is the unquenchable thirst for power.

The novel also underscored the importance of the use of words and slogans in winning people to your side. Calling the enemy terrorists and the repetition of that depiction day and night is very much like getting the people accustomed, as in Orwell's novel, to stand up every day in what is called the "Two-Minutes Hate," in which the people declare their hatred for the enemy and swear their allegiance to the regime. Orwell calls the enemy in his novel "the Brotherhood," but they could very well have been al-Qaeda or the fundamentalists. Toward the end of the novel, and during the torture sessions of the protagonist Winston, Winston asks the interrogator, O'Brien, whether the Brotherhood really exists or whether it is simply a ploy of the ruling regime. O'Brien answers, "That,

Winston, you will never know." Does that same answer apply to what is called 'al-Qaeda?'

The novel *1984* also confirms the startling readiness of people to believe what they are told, regardless of the degree to which it contradicts reason, as long as it is repeated often enough and the repetition is coupled with what Orwell calls "naïve nationalism," which incorporates blind submission to whatever the leader (Big Brother) says and the notion that the leader and the nation are one. The novel also suggests that the important thing for achieving your aims is not how things are in the real world, but what people think they are. O'Brien says to Winston during one of the torture sessions that reality is not external. It is of no importance whether two plus two equals four or five, what is important is that people be ready, once they have been sufficiently brainwashed, not simply to repeat that two plus two equals five but really to believe that it does.

The last, real victory for totalitarian governments is not to root out opposition members and to throw them in prison; it lies, rather, in changing the thoughts that run around inside their heads and in replacing them with more suitable ones. The regime depicted in Orwell's *1984* is not content just to empty out Winston's mind so that it becomes like an empty shell. The empty shell must be filled with whatever thoughts are approved of.

12

Modernization or Reform?

Since the terrible events of September 11, talk about the need for reform in the Arab world has never ceased. Conferences have been held, lectures given, and articles written, all revolving around the necessity of reform. Indeed, even military intervention was justified by the need for reform. This talk about reform has usually been mixed up with talk about modernization, as if reform were a synonym for modernization, one inconceivable without the other. Reform in the view of most writers on the subject has implicitly been taken to mean doing what some other countries have done, or catching up with them. In other words, to do what people tend to do in the more 'advanced' part of the world. If a country or government does that it will have implemented the desired reform.

A good example of this understanding of reform is to be found in what U.N. agencies have been publishing for a long time about the requirements of development in 'less-developed' countries, where endless tables are published comparing countries with each other and ranking them in such a way as to distinguish the 'advanced' from the 'less advanced.' But of course some of the best examples of this understanding of reform are the two reports published in

2002 and 2003 by the UNDP, titled *The Arab Human Development Report*, discussed earlier in this book. The two reports are a clear example of using the two concepts of reform and modernization as synonyms. As we have already seen, when the reports speak of such goals as democracy, freedom, transparency, promotion of knowledge, or the empowerment of women, they always take as their frame of reference the achievements of those countries known as the 'advanced countries,' which have 'modernized' before others. What is required of all others is merely that they catch up. And behind this view that reform and modernization are synonymous lies of course the firmly entrenched idea of 'progress.'

But what is someone like me to do, who has strong doubts about the whole notion of progress, and who abhors so many things in the modern way of life?

———

This is exactly the subject of two great novels both dealing with the problem of encounter between two cultures, one more 'modern' but not necessarily superior to the other. One has the evocative title, *Things Fall Apart*, by the Nigerian writer Chinua Achebe, which first came out in English in 1958. More than half of the novel is spent on describing the culture of a Nigerian tribe at the beginning of the last century: its customs, social ties, beliefs, and fears, what it honors and what it deplores, what it finds shameful and what it takes pride in, its cuisine, the relations between the sexes, its legends and myths. As interesting as the author makes the description, this part of the novel does not tell any story at all. The sole aim of this part, I think, is to make the reader accept the tribe, to sense the extent to which its customs, traditions, and beliefs are so intimately interlinked, and to see how every element of its culture lends meaning to life, acts as a source of self-confidence, and justifies any sacrifice that some members of the tribe may make if the sacrifice is necessary for the survival of the tribe or of its way of life. In a word, every aspect of this tribe's culture vouchsafes its survival and continuity, and no aspect can be understood and appreciated without reference to the others.

In this way, Achebe not only persuades readers of the viability of this culture but inspires in them affection for the tribe and a strong sympathy for its way of life. This having been achieved, it becomes nonsensical to try to assess each element of the culture individually, to be judged according to its utility, or to regard the culture as superior or inferior to other cultures, or to regard one part of the culture as rational and another irrational. Each element of this culture is indeed 'rational' in the way it contributes to ensuring the survival of the tribe.

Then the tragedy begins. The leader of the tribe, Okonkwo, has a son and a daughter. The girl embodies all of the qualities that Okonkwo loves and admires. She has inherited from her father his resolve and strength of will; she is loyal to her clan without reservation. The boy, on the other hand, is artless, a pale personality who lacks any of his father's physical strength, persistence, or patience in adversity. What is it that makes the boy betray his tribe and his father and to open a way for foreigners to attack his tribe and destroy it? Is it merely his weakness of character, or is it also his feeling that his father does not really love him or at least that he prefers his sister to him? We never know for sure. Whatever the reason, when the missionaries come with a foreign religion and beliefs strange to those of the tribe, the boy joins them. The father cannot believe that his own son would join the enemies of the tribe, who wish only to destroy it. It nearly drives him crazy, but the boy is obstinate, and the missionaries, backed by the guns of those wishing to appropriate the tribal lands, strengthen the boy's heart and brainwash him with the delusion that by joining them against his father and clan he will score a victory for human rights. No wonder the novel is named *Things Fall Apart*! Everything does indeed fall apart for that Nigerian tribe.

———

The other novel is *Season of Migration to the North* by the renowned Sudanese writer Tayeb Salih, which appeared for the first time in 1966. The novel still provides a credible picture of the ordeal that Arab culture is passing through in the face of the pressure of another more 'modern' culture (or civilization), one which is more youthful and vigorous as a result, but also more aggressive.

The novel describes three different attitudes toward this confrontation. The first is the attitude of those completely sold out to the West who can find no way of becoming contented with themselves except by making the West contented with them. The protagonist Mustafa Sa'eed represents this position. He learns English well and writes books in it, but he cannot find peace of mind so long as the English flirt Jean Morris refuses to accept his advances. Even after returning to his village in the Sudan, having killed Jean Morris and spent years in prison on that account, and after marrying a Sudanese girl and begetting two children with her, he still cannot forget his life in England and still painfully longs for it. He turns one of the rooms of his house into a replica of a room in an English house, with the same kind of fireplace, clippings from old English newspapers, pictures of his English girlfriends, volumes of English poetry, and so on. He ends up committing suicide.

The second attitude is that taken by those who adhere wholeheartedly to their inherited traditions and are completely free of any influence coming from the West and hence reject modernization as well as reform of any kind. This position is represented by the character Wad Rayyes, who has had no contact with the West and who, though he is over seventy with a wife and grown-up children, wants to marry a girl the age of one of his grandchildren and sees nothing shameful in this. There is nothing in his village traditions that would prevent him from having a second wife, old or young, as long as he is able to support her financially, and as long as her father agrees to the marriage, even though she had threatened to kill the prospective husband and kill herself if she was forced to marry him. Indeed, that is exactly what happens.

There is yet another exceedingly attractive character in the novel, which I take to represent the third attitude toward this ordeal of confrontation between the two cultures. He is one of the village men who seems to understand everything and recognizes the strengths and weaknesses in both the inherited as well as in the modern way of life. He loves his people and respects their customs and traditions, but he also knows what they are missing and the limits of their abilities.

Reform is needed, of course, but it must be introduced slowly, graciously, with the minimum offence to tradition.

This is the character of Mahjoub. He is quite disturbed by the new marriage of Wad Rayyes to Hosna, the young woman, and considers him a silly prattler who does not know what he is doing, but he is also greatly angered when he hears the news of Hosna killing her husband and then killing herself. In Mahjoub's view, Wad Rayyes is indeed a very foolish man who is blindly ruled by tradition, but Hosna is too reckless and rebellious, imagining that she has far more freedom than she actually does. Mahjoub is indeed a wonderful man, but unfortunately of very limited power. Like a character in a Greek tragedy, he faces an almost insoluble problem as if it foreshadows an inevitable catastrophe.

———

What in my opinion turns the problem of cultural encounter into a tragedy is not the difficulty of knowing what is the best solution or exactly which type of reform is the most desirable. The best thing is, of course, to adopt whatever is useful in modernity while retaining whatever is valuable from tradition. The problem lies rather in the fact that such an eclectic solution may not be at all feasible. There are at least two reasons to doubt its feasibility. The first is that the kind of modernization which is offered to us in the guise of reform is backed by the power of the gun. It calls us to democracy, educational reform, and the empowerment of women in an invitation coupled with a threat, which must make us very suspicious whether the goal is true democracy, real advancement of knowledge and of the position of women, or something entirely different.

It is as if we had not progressed very far since Napoleon's campaign to Egypt two centuries ago. In an attempt to justify the French invasion, Napoleon announced in a statement to the Egyptian people that he had come to rid them of "the Mamluke overlords who have ruled Egypt." He promised that "from now on, no Egyptian is to despair of assuming high office or moving up to high places. . . . The scientists and the best minds of the nation will be in charge, and this will improve the state of the nation." Then, after promising this splendid reform, his statement goes on to say, "Any village rising against French soldiers would be put to the torch."[24]

Another reason for doubting the feasibility of an eclectic solution is that the reins of power in the Arab world and the authority to make decisions about reform are for the most part in the hands of those who stand to benefit from modernization but not necessarily from real reform. That is to say, they may institute the desired model taken directly from the proponents of the modernization project, a project that mixes the good with the bad and makes no distinction between the beneficial and the harmful as it should. These power elites possess a remarkable ability—supported also by some foreign power—to stall any real reform and to prevent any genuinely free choice among alternatives. It is in their interests to portray the situation untruthfully as a struggle between the extremists, who cling to the past at any cost, and the progressive reformers, who wish to achieve progress and promote people's welfare. We have just seen however, that there is a third position that they are determined to ignore, even though it is the only position that represents true reform.

No wonder that we find Mahjoub saying toward the end of Salih's novel:

> "The world hasn't changed as much as you think. Some things have indeed changed—pumps instead of water-wheels, iron plows instead of wooden ones, sending our daughters to school, radios, cars, learning to drink whisky and beer instead of arak and millet wine—yet even so, everything's as it was." Mahjoub laughed as he said, "The world will really have changed when the likes of me become ministers in the government. And naturally that, he added still laughing, is an out-and-out impossibility."[25]

Notes

1. Francis Fukuyama, *The End of History and the New Man* (New York: The Free Press, 1992).
2. Ibn Tufayl, called Abubacer by Europeans, was an Andalusian philosopher and physician. His work *Hayy ibn Yaqzan* was a philosophical romance that described the development of a hermit, who, after long seclusion on an island, attains knowledge of the divine. The point of the work is the conflict between philosophy and religion. The book was translated into several European languages in the seventeenth century and was widely read.
3. *Khawaga* is the word used by Egyptians since the early nineteenth century to refer to people of a religion other than Islam, speaking a language other than Arabic, and wearing a hat rather than a fez or turban.
4. Al-Azhar is the principal seat of Muslim learning and the oldest continually operating institution of higher education in the world.
5. A fragrant cooking fat produced by rendering water buffalo butter.
6. Tayeb Salih, *Season of Migration to the North*, trans. Denys Johnson-Davies (Washington, D.C.: Three Continents Press, 1969), 3.
7. Ahmed Amin, *Hayati* (Cairo: al-Nahda al-Misriya, 1978) (first edition, 1950), 82. Author's translation.
8. Ibid., 151–52.
9. Those are: the traditional society, preconditions of takeoff, takeoff, drive to maturity, and high mass consumption. See Walt W. Rostow, *The Stages of Economic Growth: A Non-Communist Manifesto* (Cambridge: Cambridge University Press, 1960).
10. UNDP, *Arab Human Development Report for 2003*, Arabic edition (New York: The United Nations, 2003), 3.

11. Ibid., 10.
12. *Shorter Encyclopedia of Islam* (Leiden: Brill, 1961), 158.
13. UNDP, *Report for 2003*, 21.
14. UNDP, *Arab Human Development Report for 2002* (New York: The United Nations, 2002).
15. Ibid., page 87 of the Arabic version of the report.
16. Amartya Sen, *Development as Freedom* (New York: Alfred A. Knopf, 2000).
17. The reference here is to the propensity of many in Cairo, from street hawkers to amusement parks to mosques, to broadcast their doings by loudspeaker.
18. The second Caliph of Islam to succeed the Prophet Muhammad as the leader of the new community upon the Prophet's death.
19. Al-Hassan al-Mawardi: *Adab al-dunya wa-l-din* (Beirut: Dar al-Kutub al-'Ilmiyya, 1955), 24.
20. The Ottoman regent of Egypt (c. 1769–1849), who founded the ruling dynasty that ended in the revolution of 1952, and his grandson (1830–1895) who later served as khedive.
21. Oliver Poole, Jane Mulkerrins, and Alec Russell, "13 Seized in Anti-Terror Police Raids. Armed Swoop on Suspects in Britain as Bush Denies US Alert was Political." *The Daily Telegraph*, August 4, 2004.
22. Sonia Orwell and Ian Angus, eds., *Journalism and Letters* (London: Pelican Books, 1971), 4 vols., vol. 4, 513.
23. Aldous Huxley, *Brave New World* (London: Penguin Modern Classics [1932], 1973), 12.
24. Translated from the Arabic as cited in 'Abd al-Rahman al-Gabarty, *'Aga'ib al-athar* (Cairo: Dar al-Anwar al-Muhammadiya, no date), (Originally written in 1821) vol. 3, 6–7.
25. Salih, *Migration*, 100.